BECOMING A CHAMPION

PROVERBS DEVOTIONAL

~

A 31 DAY JOURNEY TOWARD GREATER EXCELLENCE, LEADERSHIP, AND SUCCESS

"I can't put the book down. Excellent insight and beautifully presented." ~ Patricia V.

"Each day is inspiring and uplifting - it's a guide to becoming a better you and growing your relationship with God." ~ Caryn S.

RUSS MASON

COPYRIGHT PAGE

CONTENTS

A QUICK GREETING AND INTRODUCTION | V

DAY 1 – AN AMAZING LIFE | 1

DAY 2 – DISCOVERING TREASURE | 4

DAY 3 – A LONG AND SUCCESSFUL LIFE | 7

DAY 4 – YOUR FUTURE IS BRIGHT | 10

DAY 5 – REACHING YOUR GREATEST POTENTIAL | 12

DAY 6 – UNDER PROMISE, OVER DELIVER | 14

DAY 7 – WALKING WITH WISDOM | 17

DAY 8 – LIFE, HAPPINESS, PROVISION, INFLUENCE, AND SUCCESS | 20

DAY 9 – CONTINUALLY MOVING FORWARD AND UPWARD | 23

DAY 10 – BLESSING, LEGACY, WISDOM, AND ACCOMPLISHMENT | 26

DAY 11 – DOING THE RIGHT THING | 30

DAY 12 – KIND AND DEEPLY ROOTED | 33

DAY 13 – SURROUND YOURSELF WITH CHAMPIONS | 37

DAY 14 – CONTENTMENT AND HEALTH | 40

DAY 15 – SPEAK SOFTLY AND STAY CALM | 43

DAY 16 – CONSTRUCTING A MASTERPIECE AND LEGACY | 47

DAY 17 – ENTHUSIASM AND SELF-MOTIVATION | 50

DAY 18 – HEALING, SECURITY, AND DIRECTION 53

DAY 19 – PATIENCE 56

DAY 20 – LOYALTY AND FAITHFULNESS 60

DAY 21 – ONGOING EVALUATION, MAINTENANCE, AND
    IMPROVEMENT 64

DAY 22 – SKILL AND EXCELLENCE 68

DAY 23 – MENTAL, EMOTIONAL, AND SPIRITUAL
    STABILITY 72

DAY 24 – NEVER GIVE UP 76

DAY 25 – BEAUTIFUL, PRECIOUS, AND HIGHLY VALUABLE 79

DAY 26 – SPEAK LIFE 83

DAY 27 – HUMILITY 87

DAY 28 – JOY, CELEBRATION, AND GRATITUDE 90

DAY 29 – HOPE AND EXPECTATIONS 93

DAY 30 – GOD IS IN CONTROL 97

DAY 31 – AIM HIGH 101

APPENDIX

ABOUT THE AUTHOR

CONNECT WITH RUSS MASON

YOUR FEEDBACK IS GREATLY APPRECIATED

A QUICK GREETING AND INTRODUCTION

Hello and thank you so much for choosing this devotional book about life, leadership, and becoming a champion. God has an amazing plan for your life and I hope this book will encourage, inspire, and empower you to rise higher and live at your very best each and every day. As God's precious child, you have the potential to do extraordinary things and it is my prayer that you will overcome the past, move forward, and become everything God has created you to be!

This book is the result of a tremendous season of my life in the mid to late 1990s and the years that followed. After being raised Catholic throughout my early childhood years, I began a personal and daily relationship with the Lord at a bible–based, evangelical church in 1994. Around that same time, I also became actively involved with a fantastic interdenominational Christian youth organization called Young Life. After a few years of building relationships with my adult leaders, one of them approached me in 1998 with the suggestion of reading the chapter of Proverbs that corresponds with the day of the month.

Being a young man at the time, I knew I needed more maturity, wisdom, and direction in my life so I was excited to start reading "the proverb of the day". Since calendar months have up to 31 days and there are 31 chapters in the book of Proverbs, I would encourage all Christians to add this life transforming habit to their daily Bible reading time.

The daily discipline of reading the proverb of the day since 1998 has had more of a profound impact on my personal and professional life than anyone or anything else. By reading and applying the truths and principles found in this devotional book as well as the Biblical book of Proverbs, you will see growth and lasting change in every area of your life. Little by little your work relationships, family relationships, friendships, thoughts, words, and actions will all be positively transformed. As you prayerfully read and live out everything you learn from Proverbs, your life will become wiser, brighter, fuller, stronger, more efficient, more productive, and ultimately more beautifully complete in every way. Listed below are just some of the topics we will discuss.

Living a Long and Successful Life

Reaching Your Greatest Potential

Continually Moving Forward and Upward

Surrounding Yourself with Champions

Never Giving Up

Aiming High

I'm honored and excited to have you with me on this journey of discovering your identity as God's child and transforming a little each day into the champion He has created you to be. Let the journey begin!

Day 1

An Amazing Life

~

"Let the wise listen to these proverbs and become even wiser."

Proverbs 1:5 NLT

~

"To have knowledge, you must first have reverence for the Lord."

Proverbs 1:7 GNT

God masterfully creates each person with a purpose and destiny. Even before He created the world, God knew who would live on the earth throughout the course of human history. In His eternal wisdom and sovereignty, He also designed and created each person to fulfill a unique purpose and accomplish a specific destiny. This is true for you. This is true for everyone.

So how do we discover our purpose? How do we accomplish our destiny? How do we reach our full potential? The first step is acknowledging God's existence and His supremacy throughout the whole universe. No one is greater than Him, no one is stronger than Him, and no one is wiser than Him. In order for us to reach our greatest potential and fulfill our purpose during our time on the earth, we must acknowledge God's existence and supremacy while also allowing Him to reveal to us and accomplish through us the amazing destiny He has created us to accomplish.

Since God created us, He knows us even better than we know ourselves. In addition, He loves us more than any person could. And since God is pure, He loves us unconditionally and He always has our best interest at heart.

Regardless of what you have been raised to believe, God wants you to succeed. He so passionately wants you to live an abundant and full life that is marked by His protection, favor, and blessing. God is light and He wants to shine upon you and through you. He wants your life to be pure, bright, and beautiful.

So are you ready to move forward? It's time to become and accomplish everything God has created you to be and do!

Day 1 Prayer of a Champion

"God, I acknowledge You are the God of the entire universe, that You have an amazing plan for my life, and that You created me to fulfill a specific destiny during my time on the earth. Cause me to always acknowledge You as well as include You in my life and in the decisions I make. I know You love me deeply and it is Your desire to see me prosper and succeed. Reveal Yourself to me and lead me each day one step closer to reaching my full potential and accomplishing my destiny. Amen!"

DAY 2

DISCOVERING TREASURE

~

"SEARCH FOR WISDOM AS YOU WOULD SEARCH FOR SILVER OR HIDDEN TREASURE."

PROVERBS 2:4 CEV

Have you ever watched a television show on treasure hunters? These men and women sometimes spend millions of dollars and years of their lives researching and planning for just a single expedition. First they study historical documents and maps. Then they devise the methods and strategies they will use to find the treasure. Next they brainstorm all the logistical possibilities and details of executing the treasure hunt. Then they purchase or acquire all the equipment needed to successfully bring the treasure home. And finally, once all of the planning is complete and all of the equipment is ready, they search for the earthly treasure they believe to be in a certain location.

What baffles me is all of this money, time, and energy is spent on an earthly treasure that may not even be there! Think about it. Life savings are spent and precious human lives are risked all for *possibility*, not certainty. Now imagine if we spent that same amount of money, time, and energy on a treasure we were guaranteed to not only find, but receive a benefit from every single day for the rest of our lives.

This treasure exists. It is priceless, and it is available to anyone who pays the price to search diligently for it. Finding earthly treasure is glamorous; you find a fortune and you also get the notoriety of being a successful treasure hunter. But may I suggest that finding wisdom is just as glamorous. Those who find wisdom and apply it to their everyday lives become wiser, richer, fuller, more powerful, more efficient, more productive, and more beautiful. At least to me, that sounds much more glamorous and desirable than searching through the depths of caves or oceans for something that may not be there, something that has no eternal value, and something I cannot take with me when I die.

So if not in caves and ocean floors, where do we search for and find wisdom? I believe it is found in the person of God and in the Bible – which is His Word.

Now that we know where to find wisdom, how do we search for it and attain it? I believe our active pursuit of knowing God and His Word, coupled with personal attributes such as righteousness, humility, curiosity, self–discipline, and diligence will enable our quest for wisdom to be successful.

At this point you may be asking, "Why is finding wisdom even more urgent and important than finding treasure?" In order for us to be productive, successful, and to stay on the path God has carved out for us, it is vitally important for us to listen closely to Him and also to the wise and successful leaders who have gone before us. The insight and wisdom we glean from God and these experienced individuals will help us to more efficiently navigate the turns and obstacles we will face throughout our lives.

I pray you will stay "hungry" in your pursuit of knowing God, knowing His Word, and discovering treasures of wisdom throughout your lifetime. God has an amazing plan for your life and along the way He has treasures of wisdom, knowledge, and truth that will keep you focused and on the path that leads to your greatest potential and destiny.

~

Day 2 Prayer of a Champion

"God, I thank You for placing treasures of wisdom all around me. I pray You will give me the passion and the diligence to search for the wisdom and knowledge necessary for me to live successfully and fulfill my destiny. May my heart always be soft and may my mind always be open to the wisdom and knowledge You wish to teach me along the way. Give me a deep and life–long love for Your truth, wisdom, and knowledge. I know Your wisdom and ways of doing things are the best and so help me to always seek You when I need help and understanding. Amen!"

DAY 3

A LONG AND SUCCESSFUL LIFE

~

"MY CHILD, DO NOT FORGET MY TEACHING, BUT KEEP MY COMMANDS IN MIND. THEN YOU WILL LIVE A LONG TIME, AND YOUR LIFE WILL BE SUCCESSFUL."

PROVERBS 3:1-2 NCV

So far in this devotional we have established that God loves us, He has an amazing plan for our lives, and He wants us to succeed. Now let's look at how we live a life that reflects these truths on a daily basis. In addition to searching for wisdom from the Lord and His Word, there are other sources of truth, wisdom, and knowledge we must continually draw from in order for us to accomplish our destiny and be successful. Countless individuals have lived successful lives before us, and many have journeyed a life path that is similar to the one we are currently traveling on. Because of this, there is no need for us to make all of the mistakes others have already made, nor do we need to learn all of life's lessons the hard way. There are certain lessons others have already learned, and obstacles others have already experienced and surmounted.

I realize there are certain lessons we will have to learn on our own and certain journeys we will have to travel by ourselves, but I believe God wants us to learn as much as we can from others' life experiences and obstacles so we will be spared some of the pain and damage along the way. Even by doing our best to learn from others, we will still face painful trials and seemingly impossible obstacles. This is why it is so vital for us to learn as much as we can from what others' have already experienced. There is not enough time in a lifetime to learn all of the lessons ourselves and still be as efficient, productive, and successful as God wants us to be. Because of this, our aim should be to learn as much as we can from what has already occurred throughout history so we can spend less time making our own unnecessary mistakes and more time shining bright, helping others, and fulfilling our destiny.

So who will we learn these valuable life lessons from? These verses in particular are speaking of a child learning from his biological father. In today's society, I realize this may not always be the possibility or reality for many young men and women. Since some children grow up without their biological father in the home, who should they look up to for advice and direction? I believe this principle of "remembering our father's teaching" could be applied to really anyone who is older and more experienced than us. It could be a mother, stepparent, grandparent, an older sibling, a coach, mentor, pastor, etc. The important thing to remember is whoever you go to is a person who loves God, loves you, is concerned about your life and future, and he or she has your best interest at heart. As long as what I just mentioned is true about a person, then I would say it is safe for you to listen to their advice and counsel, mix it with what God and other leaders in your life are saying, and make the best decision you can from there.

The reason I say mix their advice with what God and other leaders say is because no one is going to hear God accurately 100% of the time nor are our leaders going to be correct in their advice and counsel to us 100% of the time. By looking for the common denominator in what God and people are collectively saying, we have a much better chance of making the right decisions throughout our lives.

~

Day 3 Prayer of a Champion

"God, I'm so grateful You want me to live a long and successful life. I thank You for placing strong and wise men and women in my life who love me and want the best for me. Help me to avoid unnecessary mistakes, do my best each day to apply what I've learned from others, and to always walk in humility, integrity, and self–discipline. Help me to be careful and diligent to filter the advice of others through what You are saying and doing in my life so I stay in the center of Your will throughout my lifetime. Amen!"

DAY 4

YOUR FUTURE IS BRIGHT

~

"THE WAYS OF RIGHT-LIVING PEOPLE GLOW WITH LIGHT; THE LONGER THEY LIVE, THE BRIGHTER THEY SHINE."

PROVERBS 4:18 MSG

The sunrise – it is bright, clear, inspiring, mesmerizing, glorious, intriguing, captivating, beautiful, and wondrous. This is how God describes the life of an individual who is following Him. This is God's ideal for His people.

Many of us have heard our "glory days" (the best days of our lives), are the years when we are in high school and college. This is when we are young, energetic, independent, and free of major responsibilities. It is easy to see why many people believe this season of life is as good as it gets. God, however, says as long as we are following Him, then our lives will become brighter and more beautiful the longer we live. Amazing, isn't it?

So how is this possible? Why would God say when we are the oldest is when we will be our best and shine the brightest? I believe God says this for a few reasons.

As we follow God, we become more like God. Over time, many of our weaknesses and the unpleasant attributes of our personality are transformed into strengths and both the pleasant and beautiful attributes that reflect the personality of Almighty God. For example, as we follow God and allow His Presence and Word to transform us, we become more patient, loving, kind, gentle, and so on. As we continually follow God throughout our lives, we will also become wiser, more mature, more efficient, and more productive. Another benefit we will reap in our life–long pursuit of God is becoming both healthier and more stable spiritually, mentally, and emotionally.

So, from this perspective you can see how even in our old age, (when the world says we are past our prime), God says our prime – our best and brightest condition, is who we are right now as long as we are continually, intentionally, and passionately following Him in all we do and with all we are.

~

Day 4 Prayer of a Champion

"God, thank You for the promise that my best days are in front of me and with You my future is bright! Help me to always stay hopeful, cheerful, and positive about my life and future. Help me to become more and more like You throughout my lifetime so I can represent You well and shine bright to the world around me. May I never look back and I pray You will empower me to become wiser, stronger, and more beautiful every day and every year of my life. Amen!"

DAY 5

REACHING YOUR GREATEST POTENTIAL

~

"THEY GET LOST AND DIE BECAUSE OF THEIR FOOLISHNESS AND LACK OF SELF–CONTROL."

PROVERBS 5:23 CEV

It should be our life goal and aim to live on the opposite side of the spectrum from this verse. This verse speaks of a person who was too proud and too lazy to be self–disciplined, seek for instruction, attain wisdom and guidance from others, and ultimately reach his or her greatest potential.

May this never be said of us. This is the sad evaluation of someone who reached the end of their life and did not cultivate their gifts and become everything they could have. It should serve as a stark reminder to get as much wisdom, guidance, and instruction as we can. From books, leaders, training, and practice, we should be on a life–long journey towards self–improvement and excellence in both our personal life and in our area of expertise. This is why continual self–evaluation, self–development, and leadership training must be one of our greatest priorities in life.

It is obvious success does not just happen. It is earned through self–discipline, hard work, sacrifice, and constant learning. Even the most successful people we have heard about experienced setbacks, tragedy, and failure at some point along their journeys. What eventually made them successful, however, was their persistence, dedication, and willingness to continually learn and improve.

So let us be encouraged from this verse that learning and growing (becoming wiser, stronger, and better) is a life–long journey that will enable us to avoid the pitfalls that may jeopardize our ability to reach both our goals and our greatest potential. Choose to wake up each day and approach your life and your career with a sense of excitement, anticipation, and an ongoing willingness to learn and become better in everything you are, and in everything you do.

~

Day 5 Prayer of a Champion

"God, I thank You my life and my future are even more amazing than what I can see right now. Enable me to see my life and my future through Your eyes so I can live a life that lines up with my identity as Your child and the destiny You have created me to accomplish. Empower me to do everything possible on a daily basis to stay pure and holy so I can avoid the traps of the enemy and the pitfalls of life. Cause me to walk closely beside You so I can hear Your voice and follow Your lead each and every day. Amen!"

DAY 6

UNDER PROMISE, OVER DELIVER

~

"IF YOU'VE IMPULSIVELY PROMISED THE SHIRT OFF YOUR BACK AND NOW FIND YOURSELF SHIVERING OUT IN THE COLD, FRIEND, DON'T WASTE A MINUTE, GET YOURSELF OUT OF THAT MESS."

PROVERBS 6:2-3 MSG

It is good to be well–meaning and want to help others any way we can. The problem arises, though, when our ability to act cannot match the height of our desire to help. The remedy for this is to be discreet and wise in what we offer people. If we seek to simply be obedient to what God wants us to do in a person's life, then we will be able to fulfill our promises.

Think of it this way. It is better to simply receive a gift without prior notice than to be told a gift is coming, only to have it never arrive. Because of this, it is best for us to listen for God's voice and then give what He has instructed. Of course there will also be times when we should do things and give things simply because it is the right thing to do. When we balance these two methods of giving, we will enjoy a consistent state of confidence and peace; knowing we can deliver on what we talk about.

Even with these two methods working in balanced harmony, we still might overstep our ability to deliver on what we say at times. This is okay – no one is perfect and we must be patient with ourselves throughout the process of learning, growing, and changing. The aim of today's teaching is to help bring us closer to the side of the spectrum where we are promising less and delivering more. Instead of leaving people disappointed and with a sour taste in their mouth, we should aim to be refreshing to others because of our kind words and actions.

We are on this earth to make positive and eternal impacts on the people we interact with. We should desire to help and give as much as possible during our time on the earth. We simply must remember God is our leader and our source. Therefore, anything of eternal value we give or do for others must first come from God's will and heart, and then flow through us to other people.

So I encourage you today to allow God to fill you with His great love and compassion. As you do, your desire to serve and help others will continue to increase. He wants to fill you with great words of encouragement and wonderful deeds that will equip others to be better and help them move forward. I truly believe some of the happiest moments of our lives will be when we are joyfully blessing and helping those around us.

Day 6 Prayer of a Champion

"God, I'm so grateful You're so kind, generous, and that You are an extravagant giver. Your love compels You to continually give and do marvelous things for the people You created. Help me to promise less, give more, and to be a person that genuinely and intentionally loves and cares for others from a heart of kindness and generosity. I do not want to unnecessarily disappoint or hurt anyone so help me to hear Your voice and know exactly what You want me to say and do for others on a daily basis. Enable me to be a joy and a blessing in people's lives by giving from the overflow of Your blessing in my life. Amen!"

DAY 7

WALKING WITH WISDOM

~

"TREASURE MY CAREFUL INSTRUCTIONS. DO WHAT I SAY AND YOU'LL LIVE WELL. MY TEACHING IS AS PRECIOUS AS YOUR EYESIGHT – GUARD IT! WRITE IT OUT ON THE BACK OF YOUR HANDS; ETCH IT ON THE CHAMBERS OF YOUR HEART. TAKE THESE WORDS OF MINE MOST SERIOUSLY. TALK TO WISDOM AS TO A SISTER. TREAT INSIGHT AS YOUR COMPANION."

PROVERBS 7:1-4, 24 MSG

So far in our journey, we have learned to have reverence for the Lord, search diligently for wisdom, and acquire insight and understanding from mentors and other great leaders. Once we have all this wise counsel and godly wisdom in our lives, what should we do with it? Should we write it down in a journal and keep it safely stored on a shelf somewhere? Although that is a good first step, our pursuit and practical application of wisdom must involve much more than just that.

This proverb exhorts us to not only carry the instructions we have learned around with us everywhere we go, but to guard it as carefully as we would protect our own eyesight! Just think for a moment how carefully we protect our eyes. Even if a small particle comes close to our eye or happens to get into our eye, we are quick, careful, and determined to remove the object from our eye and get away from the source of danger as fast as possible. In light of this, let's reflect on how we can become even more diligent and careful in preserving and utilizing all of the wonderful teaching God has brought into our lives.

Have you ever been standing somewhere and didn't want to forget something so you wrote it on the back of your hand? Maybe it was a name, phone number, email address, or something you didn't want to forget to purchase at the store. In the same way, when we metaphorically write what we have learned on the back of our hands (by memorizing it and having it ready in our minds at all times), we will be prepared to wisely and successfully handle life's difficult and delicate situations.

In the second part of this verse, we are exhorted to speak to wisdom like we would a sister and to treat insight like a companion. I believe this verse is saying we must appreciate, value, and keep the advice of our mentors and leaders as close to us as we would a relative or dear friend. Wisdom is not something only gray headed grandfathers and grandmothers have. All of us, regardless of our age, education, or experience, should do our best to attain as much wisdom, guidance, and instruction as we can – as early and as often as we can.

Both young children and teens should remain receptive to the wise instruction and guidance of their relatives and leaders. Their disposition toward life and learning should be one that keeps them humble, teachable, and passionate enough about becoming better that they listen to the advice of their teachers, coaches, pastors, and other community leaders.

Regarding adults, there is always room for improvement and since information and technology is constantly changing and advancing, they should also continually seek the counsel of older men and women who have greater wisdom and experience.

When we attain wisdom, guard what we have learned, and keep those instructions as close to us as we would a relative or close friend, we exponentially increase our probability of success in both our personal and professional lives.

~

Day 7 Prayer of a Champion

"God, thank You for the valuable wisdom and the precious people You have placed in my life. Help me to appreciate and highly value my leaders and the wisdom they speak into my life. Empower me to keep their counsel close to me at all times and to guard it as carefully as I would guard my own eyes. May I remember the advice and wisdom I attain, and help me to use it to successfully navigate the situations and circumstances of my life. Amen!"

DAY 8

LIFE, HAPPINESS, PROVISION, INFLUENCE, AND SUCCESS

~

"RICHES AND HONOR ARE MINE TO GIVE. SO ARE WEALTH AND LASTING SUCCESS. WHAT I GIVE IS BETTER THAN THE FINEST GOLD, BETTER THAN THE PUREST SILVER. HAPPY ARE THOSE WHO LISTEN TO ME. THOSE WHO FIND ME FIND LIFE, AND THE LORD WILL BE PLEASED WITH THEM."

PROVERBS 8:18-19, 34-35 NCV

Everyone wants to be happy, taken care of, and successful throughout their endeavors and lifetime. The problem, however, is how people go about attaining these things. Many people pursue happiness to get happiness, they pursue wealth to get wealth, and they pursue success to get success. This formula, however, is unreliable and not in harmony with God's ways of living life to the fullest. Many can attest to the fact that chasing after these things with impure motives usually only leads to frustration and heartache. God's ways, however, always lead to joy, peace, and eternal satisfaction.

So let's look at God's ways of attaining happiness, wealth, and success throughout the duration of our lives. It's important for us to first establish that personal happiness, wealth, and success are good things as long as we attain and possess them in a way that is Biblical and pleasing to God. Since we are God's children as well as His representatives on the earth, we should be the ones who are entrusted with the resources necessary to influence and change the world He created. If it is true we are alive on the earth to shine for God and to influence the world for Him, then it makes perfect sense He would give us the influence and resources necessary to bring about the changes He wishes to see.

The world says to pursue happiness, wealth, and success and to go straight after them with feverous determination. God, however, says to humbly pursue wisdom and the values of His Kingdom and everything else will be given to us as well. This takes great faith. To let go of the things we need and want in order to simply pursue God's divine and eternal wisdom. But this pursuit is worth every minute we take and every effort we make.

God is our good, heavenly Father. He wishes for us to be taken care of – provided for in every area and in every way. He also wishes for us to be filled with heavenly joy and peace that will last throughout this life and all eternity. This kind of joy and peace is deep and constant, which means it does not drastically fluctuate with the ever changing circumstances of our lives.

So what have we been pursuing? Are we desperately grasping after the things of this world, hoping they will provide the things only God can truly give us? Chasing after these things outside of God's will and purpose is exhausting. God, however, wants you to live in a continual state of peace, joy, and contentment. When we pursue Him and His great wisdom, He promises to not only take care of us in every way imaginable, He also promises to fill our journey with the inexpressible joy and peace that only He can provide.

~

Day 8 Prayer of a Champion

"God, I'm so grateful You are my good, heavenly Father and that You desire to not only take care of me, but to also see me succeed and be full of abundant joy and peace. Help me to remember that true provision, joy, and success can only come from You. Cause me to live for You and to make knowing You and the ways of Your Kingdom my number one priority. Thank You for all of Your many promises, especially the one to always be with me and always take care of me. I love You, I trust You, and I am so excited to live the rest of my life alongside of You. Amen!"

DAY 9

CONTINUALLY MOVING FORWARD AND UPWARD

~

"IF YOU HAVE GOOD SENSE, INSTRUCTION WILL HELP YOU TO HAVE EVEN BETTER SENSE. AND IF YOU LIVE RIGHT, EDUCATION WILL HELP YOU TO KNOW EVEN MORE."

PROVERBS 9:9 CEV

~

"IT'S THROUGH ME, LADY WISDOM, THAT YOUR LIFE DEEPENS, AND THE YEARS OF YOUR LIFE RIPEN."

PROVERBS 9:11 MSG

Life is an adventurous journey. It is about continually moving forward and upward each day toward our eventual return to Heaven. Like life, attaining greater wisdom, excellence, success, and leadership is a continual journey. No matter how wise, excellent, efficient, or productive we become, there will always be more to learn; and we can always become even better than we are today.

Like a young child, we should approach our life, the world, and our future with a sense of awe and wonder. The earth and its people are so beautiful and amazing in so many ways. There is so much to explore and discover that we could not possibly do or learn it all during one lifetime.

What we can do, however, is explore and discover as much as we possibly can each day. One of the most important things we can do throughout our lifetime is maintain a tender heart and an open mind. The reason I alluded to a young child earlier is because they are innocent, humble, and teachable. They are excited about new adventures and they are willing to try new things in order to add to their knowledge and life experiences.

So how do we do this? Some practical and easy ways are to read books, watch documentaries on various people and topics, and to mingle with people outside of our immediate industry and circle of friends. Another great way to continually learn and grow is to travel when possible. Traveling expands our worldview and it enables us to see the world and people through a much richer and broader lens.

In light of all this, let's continually remind ourselves how brief and precious life really is. Let's also decide that we will be passionate learners of everything we can, and that we will grow and become a little better each day. To accomplish this, it is vital we do our best to always maintain a tender heart and an open mind – regardless of what happens to us or around us.

God has created and provided so many amazing people and things throughout this world that we can learn and grow from. Make it your life aim to experience as much as possible so you can better yourself and become everything He has created you to be.

~

Day 9 Prayer of a Champion

"God, I thank You for this beautiful world and all the amazing people You have so marvelously created. Help me to never lose my sense of awe and wonder and may I always be excited about learning and growing. Cause me to approach each day with joyful anticipation and a passion to be better. Open my eyes to see the wonder of life and the beauty all around me. May everyone I meet and every experience I have make my life fuller and richer. Empower me to always keep my eyes on You and to continually move forward and upward toward my destiny. Amen!"

DAY 10

BLESSING, LEGACY, WISDOM, AND ACCOMPLISHMENT

~

"BLESSINGS CROWN THE HEAD OF THE RIGHTEOUS."

"THE MEMORY OF THE RIGHTEOUS WILL BE A BLESSING."

"THE MOUTH OF THE RIGHTEOUS IS A FOUNTAIN OF LIFE AND THEIR LIPS NOURISH MANY."

"WHAT THE RIGHTEOUS DESIRE WILL BE GRANTED."

PROVERBS 10:6, 7, 11, 21, 24 NIV

———————————

There are so many promises for the righteous in the book of Proverbs. Now when you think of being righteous, try not to think of it from a traditionally religious perspective. To be righteous simply means to live in a way that makes God smile – to love Him and to love people. If how we are living on a daily basis makes God proud and happy of us, then we are righteous. To be clear, though, God loves everyone the same. His love does not change with our righteousness or lack thereof. What does change, is what happens to us and through us. By living a righteous life, we attract God's favor, blessing, and promotion. Not only that, we also become channels through which God can flow to the people around us.

God wants to bless you and He really enjoys doing good things for you. Like a good dad, God loves to spoil His children. That is why in verse six it says God's children will wear His blessings like a crown. Throughout the centuries, the crown has been a distinguishing symbol of beauty, honor, leadership, victory, and influence. Like a proud dad, God wants to distinguish you and show the world you are both His child and that He dearly loves you.

Looking now at verse seven, God says the memory of the righteous will be a blessing. Although it takes a lifetime for a legacy to be established, it is pieced together a little each day through our words and actions. This is why it is vitally important for us to live our lives through the lens of eternity. What are we doing today that will live on after we are gone? God wants our lives to outlive us. In other words, we should live in such a way that our words and actions have a positive, tangible, and an eternal influence on the people we interact with. Let's live intentionally, with purpose and destiny always in mind. God wants the memory of your life to bless and inspire future generations so live each day to the fullest; knowing your lasting legacy is always being constructed.

Tying in to legacy, verses 11 and 21 say the mouth of the righteous is a fountain of life and that their words nourish many. Is this true of our mouth and words? Our words are so very powerful. Whether we realize it or not, they are actually helping to steer the course of both our lives and the lives we have influence over. Because of this, it is imperative for us to always be aware of what we are saying to both ourselves and those around us. These two verses are God's ideal for His people and we should do our best to live up to them. Regardless of how others are speaking around you or to you, determine that you will be a fountain of life and that your words will be a continual source of hope, encouragement, and blessing.

Finally in verse 24, this chapter of Proverbs says what the righteous desire will be granted. As we grow in our relationship with the Lord, our desires, goals, and dreams become more and more aligned with God's perfect plan for our lives. Because of this, God gladly gives us both what we need for our journey while also blessing us with things simply for our enjoyment. Again this sounds like how a great dad treats his children, doesn't it? So what are you hoping for? What are you dreaming for? Allow God to show you His perfect plan and live each day with a childlike expectancy that is ready to go on the next big adventure with dad. He has so many wonderful things to show you, give you, and accomplish through you!

Day 10 Prayer of a Champion

"God, I thank You that more than anything, You simply desire a daily and vibrant relationship with me. Empower me to live in such a way that brings a smile to Your face and makes You proud and happy. It's so overwhelming that You desire to even CROWN me with Your blessings. You are so good to me and I simply ask You to teach me to handle and utilize the blessings You give to me in a way that honors and pleases You. I know one day my life will come to an end and so I pray the memory of my life in the minds of others will be a blessing and a source of inspiration for future generations. I also recognize the power of my words and the influence they have on others and so I pray You will guard my mouth and cause my words to be a source of encouragement and blessing to those who hear me. I desire to always follow You and so cause my hopes and dreams to become more and more aligned with Your perfect plan for my life. I love You and again I thank You for the many blessings You wish to bring into my life. Amen!"

Day 11

Doing the Right Thing

~

"The merciful, kind, and generous man benefits
himself [for his deeds return to bless him]."

Proverbs 11:17 AMP

~

"If your goals are good, you will be respected."

Proverbs 11:27 GNT

~

"If you do what is right, you are certain to be
rewarded."

Proverbs 11:18 GNT

Doing the right thing – it is a phrase we hear people say
but what does it mean exactly? I believe it all boils
down to choices. Throughout each day, we all
encounter dozens of moments when we are faced with
choices regarding what we will think, say, and do.
When we talk about doing the right thing, I believe it is

us making the best possible choice in each of those moments. And when we say best possible choice, best for whom? The answer is the key to today's teaching.

Doing the right thing means we make choices with a heart of compassion, mercy, and kindness for the world around us. Doing the right thing also means our choices will leave a particular person, organization, or situation better than before. It means we make choices with God, others, and the whole of society in mind. In order to do the right thing, we must ask ourselves, "What will create a better today and a better future for me and others?" In addition, doing the right thing must prompt us to ask, "What choice best represents the heart and character of God?" As we run our daily choices through these filters, we will find ourselves able to consistently live with a clear conscience – which in turn will enable us to live healthy and sleep well at night. Doing the right thing will also enable us to walk through life with great confidence and peace; knowing we do our best each day to love others and leave people, organizations, and situations better than how we find them.

The ability to live this way is absolutely priceless! To live on a regular basis (regardless of what we face in life), with a pure heart and mind is worth more than having millions in the bank. As the verses state, when we choose to do good from a heart of mercy, kindness, and generosity, we actually bring good back upon ourselves. So, if you want a healthier, fuller, and more peaceful life, make your choices based on love and the character of God; without worrying about being right or getting even. God will settle the score. He will defend you and make sure you are taken care of. All we must do is our best each day to choose what is right in the eyes of God and as the above verses say, we will benefit ourselves and be rewarded by our amazing heavenly Father.

~

Day 11 Prayer of a Champion

"God, I'm so grateful You make choices from Your heart of love, compassion, and generosity. Enable me to see myself, others, and the daily situations I face through Your eyes and with Your heart. I wish to leave people, organizations, and situations better than how I found them so empower me to make excellent choices that will mutually benefit everyone involved. Cause me to walk uprightly with a heart of integrity and do the right thing to the best of my ability. I long to be like You and I thank You for being such an awesome example to me. Amen!"

DAY 12

KIND AND DEEPLY ROOTED

~

"GOOD PEOPLE HAVE KIND THOUGHTS."

PROVERBS 12:5 CEV

~

"GOOD PEOPLE ARE LIKE TREES WITH DEEP ROOTS."

PROVERBS 12:12 CEV

The book of Proverbs is like a litmus test for our lives. If you ever want to know if you are living up to God's standard of wisdom and excellence, all you have to do is reflectively read Proverbs and see if your daily life aligns with the verses you are reading. Today, let's see if our lives match the litmus test of kindness, having deep roots, and loving others.

Our minds and thoughts are very powerful. If we are honest, they actually define who we are and how we perceive the world around us. So what does it mean to have kind thoughts? I believe it means to think positively; but more than that, I believe to have kind thoughts means we do our very best to think, assume, and believe the best about people and situations. This of course is a general rule we should apply to most of the people, most of the time. This does not mean we sugar coat or dismiss evil people or situations. There is certainly blatant evil in the world and it should be thought of as such and dealt with as such. Overall, however, our state of mind and our continual thought processes should remain positive, loving, kind, and even innocent. This will allow us to remain calm and in a state of consistent peace and rest. God does not want us living in a state of worry, fear, anxiety, hate, or turmoil. People who live this way are dying a slow death. Their thoughts are slowly killing them like a cancer from the inside out. God, however, wants you to live a life that is filled with hope, joy, peace, love, and strength. He wants both your mind and your body to be robust and vibrantly healthy so you can live powerfully and effectively for Him.

Another attribute of a good person is they have deep roots. The best way for us to apply this to our everyday lives is to simply think of a tall and healthy tree. What do its roots do? A tall and healthy tree's roots provide stability, security, and nourishment for itself – and if you think about it, you'll realize a tree's roots ultimately benefit more than just itself. A tree's roots allow its leaves and fruit to grow, which in turn provide shade and food for other living things. In the same way, when we have deep roots in God and His Word, we will also be stable, secure, nourished, and able to provide "shade" and "food" for others.

Let's take a closer look at each of these components. When it comes to stability and security, a tree's roots protect it from falling over during the storms it must weather. Likewise, when we are deeply rooted in God, we will be able to successfully withstand the various storms of life we will inevitably face. When it comes to being nourished, a tree cannot be healthy, nor can it provide shade and food to other living things unless it receives a consistent flow of necessary nutrients through its trunk and branches. This same truth applies to us as well. In order for us to stay consistently strong and healthy throughout the many seasons of life, we must receive from God all the intangible nutrients that keep a person spiritually, mentally, emotionally, and physically strong. Then, out of the overflow of our strength and health, we will be able to provide "shade" and "food" to those around us. Shade provides coolness in the heat of summer – it both protects and refreshes. Metaphorically, we are also created by God to protect, refresh, and keep others cool as they pass within our shade. When it comes to providing "food", this could be interpreted in the literal sense but I also believe we are to provide intangible nutrition for others – much like God does for us. Things like love, encouragement, and advice are what come to mind when I think about the intangible "nutrients" we as humans provide for one another.

So, with all of this in mind, be very aware of your thoughts throughout the day and make sure they stay continually loving and kind. In addition, be aware of the role God wants you to fulfill on the earth and know part of that role is to be so rooted in Him that you are stable and strong enough to stand tall for yourself while also providing shade and nutrients to those who come close to you.

~

Day 12 Prayer of a Champion

"God, thank You once again for being such a wonderful example to me. Thank You for having kind thoughts and feelings toward me and humanity as a whole. Teach me to be disciplined in my mind and to keep my thoughts loving and kind toward You, myself, and those around me. In addition, empower me to do my best every day to think, assume, and believe the best about people and the situations I face. Since it is Your will for me to be strong and stable, cause me to stay rooted in You all the days of my life so I can successfully weather the storms I will face. Help me be mindful of those around me and enable me to be so stable and healthy that I can provide "shade" and "food" to those who come near me. I love You and I'm so grateful that in You I am strong and safe for all eternity. Amen!"

Day 13

Surround Yourself with Champions

~

"Spend time with the wise and you will become wise."

Proverbs 13:20 NCV

———————————

There is no doubt to some extent we are a product of our environment. Even if we have a strong personality that is not easily influenced, to some degree we will still emulate those we spend most of our time with. Therefore, if we want to become a champion, then we need to spend time with other champions.

This is true for any area of life. Whether it's academics, athletics, or in our professional careers, we will start to speak, act, and perform like those we learn, practice, and work with. Of course we should seek to be most heavily influenced by our relationship with the Lord and His Word, but we must also carefully select who we will allow to be in our inner circle; i.e. the people we spend the most amount of time with and those with whom we are the most transparent and vulnerable. When we let our guard down and allow others to speak into our lives, this is when we are the most pliable and easily influenced.

Life is a journey and along the journey we must continually learn, grow, and adapt to our surroundings. The world, its people, and the environments we live and work in are constantly changing. Because of this, we must be willing and ready to make the necessary adjustments in order to stay as sharp, efficient, and productive as possible. Since the world and our environments constantly change, our influencers and mentors should also change as our lives and careers evolve. As you are promoted into different roles and areas of expertise throughout your career, you should be continually scanning the horizon for the next great champion God will bring into your life.

Remember, forward and upward is God's will for your life – so never settle for standing still or maintaining your current level of excellence, leadership, or productivity. God has greater opportunities and blessings for you to both seize and receive. Therefore, never settle or look back. Live each day looking ahead with excitement and anticipation for what God wants to accomplish in you and through you. The champions in your life will help you both see and attain the great things God has planned for you.

So, with all of this in mind, ask God to surround you with champions and bring the right people into your life. Look around for the people in your industry who are moving forward and accomplishing the things you hope to accomplish one day. Find the winners and make room for them in your circle of friends and influencers. These individuals should be men and women of integrity and character who are positive, persistent, and hardworking. By surrounding yourself with individuals like this and walking beside them on the journey of life, you further assure your success as you venture forward.

~

Day 13 Prayer of a Champion

"God, I thank You for being the greatest champion of all and the best possible example for me to follow. I'm so grateful You have already selected amazing men and women who will walk beside me through different seasons of my life. Enable me to recognize them and invite them to be in my life so I can continually move forward and reach my greatest potential. I pray You will remove anyone from my life who is holding me back and keeping me from fulfilling my destiny. Give me wisdom to know who needs to be in my life and cause me to make room for more champions. Amen!"

Day 14

Contentment and Health

~

"The tent of the upright will flourish."

Proverbs 14:11 NIV

~

"A calm and undisturbed mind and heart are the life and health of the body."

Proverbs 14:30 AMP

Contentment, peace, and overall abundance in every area of your life – this is what God wants for you. God is a loving, compassionate, and generous father who wants to bless us and see us prosper and succeed throughout our lifetime. What I love about verse 11 is regardless of our material possessions, God says our lives will flourish. I believe He says this because flourishing has to do with much more than just our material possessions. Many people in the world today have homes, cars, and millions in the bank, but they are completely bankrupt when it comes to love, joy, peace, and overall contentment. Regardless of what they accomplish or attain, they are perpetually unfulfilled when it comes to who they are and what they have. God, however, wants people to flourish, thrive, and be blessed from the inside out. When God blesses us with material possessions, it should simply be an overflow of the immaterial blessings He has already filled us with on the inside.

If we are rich in things like love, joy, peace, and contentment, then we are truly rich indeed. When we talk about abundance and prosperity, it must begin with these intangibles. To have material possessions without love, joy, peace, and contentment is like giving a priceless family heirloom to a young child. Since the child is still immature and unable to fully understand the heritage of the family heirloom, he or she cannot responsibly handle or fully appreciate its rich history and priceless worth. So it is with us. God must make us rich in love, joy, peace, and contentment before we will be able to properly appreciate and handle the spiritual and material blessings He wants to bring into our lives.

You may have heard it said that if we don't have our health then we don't have anything. This is so true because if we aren't healthy, then we cannot work, play, or enjoy the things we have worked so hard to attain. Just as we should do all we can to ward off sickness and disease, we should continually be aware of the emotional diseases that are just as capable of killing us – both metaphorically and literally. Things like jealousy, anger, and hatred will slowly destroy us much like a terminal disease will.

When it comes to personal health, many people run to the gym and/or the latest diet in order to lose weight and get stronger. Although it is vitally important to exercise and eat healthy, we must be diligent in pursuing health in our thoughts and emotions as well; for they also have a tremendous influence on our physical health. When our minds are at rest and our emotions are at peace, our physical bodies are able to function and even thrive the way God intends.

As we begin each day, let's choose to live according to God's Word, maintain a position of rest and peace in both our thoughts and emotions, and do our best to be content with who we are and what we have. If we will do this, we will flourish and live the lives of abundant peace and health God created us to both live and enjoy.

~

Day 14 Prayer of a Champion

"God, I'm so grateful Your desire is for me to flourish and Your will for my life is abundant peace, joy, and overall contentment. Help me to be thankful and to appreciate everything I have. I know both my material possessions and my mental, emotional, and spiritual health all come from You. Cause me to trust You and stay close to You so I can experience and enjoy a continual state of rest, peace, and contentment. Throughout my life, empower me to steer clear of emotional diseases and help me to keep my thoughts, words, and actions aligned with both You and Your Word. Thank You for taking care of me and causing me to flourish regardless of my circumstances. Amen!"

Day 15

Speak Softly and Stay Calm

~

"A gentle response defuses anger."

Proverbs 15:1 MSG

~

"A calm, cool spirit keeps the peace."

Proverbs 15:18 MSG

Amidst our daily routines and interactions, it can feel at times like our lives are being overrun by busyness, noise, and even chaos. Because of this, words like gentle and calm can sound more like a fantasy world than a way to describe our personal disposition. But since the world and its people are moving at such a frantic pace, remaining gentle and calm is the exact recipe and strategy God has provided for us to successfully navigate the tumultuous environments we pass through on a daily basis. Work, traffic, the gym, the grocery store, even interacting with our close family and friends at times, life can be ferocious and if we are not trained to handle life according to God's Word, we may find ourselves getting eaten alive and/or responding in a way we are not proud of. This is not God's best for us.

What God truly wants is for us to be victorious and peaceful even in the seemingly insignificant moments throughout our daily routines. When the rest of the world gets stressed and responds out of frustration and anger, God wants us to remain peaceful and respond out of a heart that is filled with His love, gentleness, and peace. Although this might sound difficult and even impossible for some of us, I assure you it is God's best and it is God's ideal for handling the inevitable turmoil we all face on a daily basis as we pursue our dreams.

My challenge for us today is for us to intentionally choose to live above the storms of life where the gusts of wind and the bolts of lightning cannot even touch us. Stay as close to God as you can – He is in control and He lives in a continual state of peace and rest. He knows all of eternity from beginning to end and so He doesn't get worked up over little things like we do. How immeasurably our daily lives will improve once we learn to respond like He does. In addition, since God is so secure and confident, we will also benefit greatly to know who we are as His child. Choose to face each day standing tall and with full confidence; knowing God is big enough to both defend and vindicate you. For He has already fought and won our battles and so all we have to do is rest in His power and receive the victory. As you go through each day, remain in that place of victory and do not allow someone else to take away your love, joy, and peace.

Regardless of what others say and do, choose to stay loving, calm, and peaceful. This is the key to maintaining a continual state of peace and rest throughout the duration of your lifetime. Life is too short to fight every single battle that arises around us on a daily basis. For sure, if we spend most of our time and energy trying to be right, proving others wrong, and winning every argument and battle we come across, that is all we would ever do. We only have so much mental and emotional energy each day and so we must be very careful to preserve and use that energy for things that truly matter and for working toward accomplishing our goals. God has an amazing plan for your life and an extraordinary destiny for you to fulfill. Instead of wasting your time and energy trying to win every single battle, focus on winning the overall war (reaching your greatest potential and fulfilling your destiny).

So in conclusion to today's teaching, lift your eyes from what is petty and begin to see the big picture of your life through the lens of eternity. This will enable you to stay secure in who you are as God's child and to know what battles are worth fighting. While the rest of the world is spinning a million miles an hour, I pray you will enjoy each day of your life by rising above the storms and living in a consistent state of love, rest, and peace.

Day 15 Prayer of a Champion

"God, I'm so grateful You are secure and You live in a continual state of peace and rest. Regardless of what is happening to me or around me, enable me to be like You by remaining calm and responding from a heart that is filled with Your love and gentleness. Empower me to rise above the storms I face and hide myself in You. Teach me to not get stressed about the small and petty things of life and keep me from fighting battles that do not matter. I realize the most important thing is reaching my greatest potential and fulfilling my destiny so remind me to stay focused on the big picture and to view my life through the lens of eternity. Amen!"

DAY 16

CONSTRUCTING A MASTERPIECE AND LEGACY

~

"IT IS BETTER TO BE PATIENT THAN POWERFUL. IT IS BETTER TO WIN CONTROL OVER YOURSELF THAN OVER WHOLE CITIES."

PROVERBS 16:32 GNT

What are we building with our lives? If we desire to be champions for God and reach our full potential, then we are also determined to build a beautiful legacy during our time on the earth. That is, we hope to reach the end of our lives confident that our influence will live on and that during our life, we accomplished something of value that positively impacted our generation and our world.

But before we can change the world, we must first be willing to allow ourselves to be changed.

Before we can lead, teach, and help others, we must first allow God and others to lead, teach, and help us overcome the past, discover our identity, and begin to take steps forward toward our God–given destiny.

It is a noble desire to want to "build" something with our life that will last beyond our lifetime. For this to be accomplished, we must first take the time to plan, prepare, dig deep, and build a strong foundation that can support the legacy we hope to build.

Many people, as they grow up and become adults, want power, influence, and control over schools, corporations, communities, and even entire nations. But God is looking for those who will first take the extra time to seek Him so they can know what their true identity and destiny is as God's child. God wants you to accomplish amazing things even more than you wish to. He even planned each one of your days before He created the world. He has been waiting for you to show up on the scene and here you are! Now that you're here, don't waste time chasing power and control over things God never intended for you to have. If you do, you will find you spent your whole life feverously clawing your way up a ladder that does not lead to your God–given destiny.

Since God created you and loves you more than any other person, allow Him to show you what you have been uniquely designed to accomplish. I can assure you His plan is even more amazing, fulfilling, and satisfying than what you are dreaming of.

Once you know what God is calling you to accomplish in life, then the next step is to allow Him to train you and prepare you for what you will be remembered for. During this process, be patient and remind yourself that God's ways and timing are perfect. Once you are spiritually mature, properly trained, and the timing for you to be released is just right, God will promote you and open the right doors for you to enter into the fullness of your calling and destiny. Simply approach each day with a desire to know Him better and to follow His lead in everything you do. Allow God and those He brings into your life to "build" you by leading, teaching, and helping you to become as strong and beautiful as possible. As you allow Him to build you into the masterpiece you were created to be, He will allow you to start building the legacy He created you to leave behind. As we walk with Him, God will direct our steps and day by day we will get closer to living out on a daily basis the amazing destiny we were created for.

~

Day 16 Prayer of a Champion

"God, I thank You that even before the world began, You decided to give me the opportunity to live on the earth and fulfill an amazing destiny. Cause me to climb the right "ladder" so I live the life and reach the levels of effectiveness and productivity You created me to. Empower me to attain control and success over my own mind and body so I will be stable and strong enough to do everything You desire. I want to leave a beautiful legacy behind so please help me to allow both you and others to guide me down the right path. Lead me a little closer each day to reaching my full potential and fulfilling every purpose and plan You have destined me for. Amen!"

Day 17

Enthusiasm and Self-Motivation

~

"A hard-working slave will be placed in charge of a no-good child, and that slave will be given the same inheritance that each child receives."

Proverbs 17:2 CEV

Success is not limited by a person's title, it is limited by a person's attributes such as their enthusiasm and excellence. If you want a promotion, all you have to do is start thinking, talking, and acting like you already have it. Before long, your superiors will recognize your self-motivation and diligence and they will elevate you to the place where your performance matches your title and salary. Some of you may be wondering, "What if my current employer doesn't recognize my excellence and hard work?" The good news is, even if your employer does not recognize and promote you, God sees your hard work and excellence. He will reward you even if it means moving you to a different department, company, or even to a new career.

Do not limit your future based on what you think is likely or possible. God knows where we need to be and where we deserve to be and He is amazing at closing the wrong doors and opening the right ones. Keep doing your best on a daily basis and work with a sense of diligence and honor no matter who you are working with or for. As you do this, God will promote you into the next season of your life.

At times you may feel like you are waiting too long. When you feel this way, simply remind yourself God is molding you and teaching you very valuable lessons about life and people through the environment and season you are in right now. He has you where you are so you can grow and mature in the areas you will need to have mastered in order to be successful in the next season of your life.

God does not want you going into the next season of your life and career unprepared and ill–equipped. He wants the transition from this season of your life to the next one to be a graduation, elevation, and promotion. If this is true, then we must pass all the "tests" and graduate from the "school" He currently has us in. Allow me to encourage you today to not give up or drop out of the "school" God has you in right now. Learn the lessons, master the concepts, and allow Him to fully prepare and equip you through your current environment and season. This will make you stronger and better prepared to climb and conquer the next mountain God brings you to.

Do not look around and do not worry about what others are or aren't doing. Simply do your best each day with enthusiasm and excellence – knowing God is watching you, He has an amazing plan for your life, and

He wants to elevate and promote you to the next level. The wonderful news is life with God is a continual progression forward and upward. Because of this, every time we graduate from one season to the next, we are getting one step closer to being the fully mature and alive person God created us to be. In addition, we are also getting one step closer to fulfilling the incredible destiny we were created to accomplish.

~

Day 17 Prayer of a Champion

"God, I'm so grateful that with You in my life there are no limits. You are in control and You are the One who opens doors for me and promotes me. Empower me and cause me to be enthusiastic and self–motivated every day of my life regardless of where I am working or who I am working for. I trust You and I know You wish to promote me to the next season of my life. Help me to be patient and to successfully pass all of the "tests" I will face. I recognize You are preparing me for an amazing destiny and so I ask You to teach me the lessons and help me master the concepts I will need to be successful and reach my greatest potential. I love You and I am so excited to be my best each day and to eventually graduate into the next season of life and level of leadership You have planned for me. Amen!"

Day 18

Healing, Security, and Direction

~

"The LORD is a mighty tower where his people can run for safety."

Proverbs 18:10 CEV

What do we run to when we feel afraid, lost, disappointed, frustrated, sad, or upset about something? We were designed and created to run to the One who made us; the One who truly knows us and loves us more than anyone else can or will. Like an engineer and the car he designs, God knows every single part of us thoroughly and perfectly – spiritual, mental, emotional, and physical. Since He knows us so intricately, He also knows exactly how to fix us when we are worn down or broken.

Unfortunately, people who are in pain or trouble often run to things that just cause more damage, pain, and shame in the long run. The result of running to God, however, is life, healing, and restoration. So again, what are we running to? In God's presence are life, hope, healing, restoration, identity, purpose, peace, and fullness of joy. Determine in your mind and heart that whenever you experience negativity in your thoughts and emotions you will run to God; for He has everything we are looking for and everything we need.

Think of it this way. When a soldier is wounded on the battlefield, he does not stay in the midst of his enemies to incur further harm and damage. Rather, he removes himself from the presence of danger and hides himself away for a while so he can recover and regain his strength. Once this time of healing is complete, then he is ready and able to go back out and fight some more. So, when you get wounded on the battlefield of life, do not stay out on the battlefield in the midst of danger, trying to bandage your own wounds. Instead, run to God and spend some time resting in His presence so He can heal you and make you strong again.

The other critical time when we should run to God is when we feel lost or afraid concerning the future. When someone climbs a tower, they have a great advantage because they are safe from enemies on the ground, plus they can see further across the horizon and get a better understanding of the land's topography. So it is with God and our lives. When we run to God for safety and direction, He will not allow our enemies to harm us and He will also provide us with a better vantage point for our life and future by enabling us to see further across the horizon than if we were standing at ground level. May it comfort you to know that you don't have to figure it all out by yourself and know exactly how to get to where God is calling you. God sees your whole life as a single snapshot and

He will reveal to you which direction to take and which strategy to use as you venture forward into the unknown future toward fulfilling your destiny.

~

Day 18 Prayer of a Champion

"God, I'm so grateful You know me perfectly and are able to heal me when I am worn down, hurt, or broken. When I am in need of healing, keep me from running to the wrong things and cause me to run to You, Your presence, and Your Word. I know You have everything I need and so help me to remember You are the only One who can truly heal me and fill me. When I am lost and confused, lift me higher so I can see things from Your perspective. I am so grateful You will always show me which direction to take and which strategy to use as I venture forward toward my destiny. You're the best, God. Thank You for being the mighty tower I can run to for safety, healing, and direction. Amen!"

DAY 19

PATIENCE

~

"WILLINGNESS AND STUPIDITY DON'T GO WELL TOGETHER. IF YOU ARE TOO EAGER, YOU WILL MISS THE ROAD."

PROVERBS 19:2 CEV

God loves people who are willing and ready to go anywhere and do anything for Him. But God also loves people who are humbly and obediently able to go when He says, "Go", and wait when He says, "Wait".

Although we all want to reach our highest potential and be operating in the fullness of our calling and destiny, God has to be the One who promotes us and opens the right doors for us. Since we as Christians are all living and serving within the realm of God's Kingdom, He knows when to release certain people into their destiny and when certain people need further training and preparation.

Throughout the Bible, you'll find instances when individuals thought God was late in His timing. Rather than humbly wait for God to move on their behalf, they tried to force God's plan by hastily acting out of their own will, strength, and timing. Even after these individuals acted out of impatience and consequential mistakes were made, they still had to wait for God to bring about His plan and purpose in His perfect way and timing. Therefore, let us learn from these examples in the Bible and realize it would be much better for us to continue to wait and trust the Lord to do things His way and according to His timetable.

God sees you and He knows what you are going through. He knows it is difficult to wait, but you can trust that while you are waiting, He is further strengthening you and preparing you for your destiny. On the days when it seems like it is never going to happen, remind yourself that God wants you to bear much fruit and to be flourishing and thriving in the fullness of your calling and destiny even more than you do.

So what happens while we are waiting? God is cleansing us, healing us, restoring us, empowering us, and equipping us. He is taking out of us bad memories, experiences, and habits and replacing them with His love, peace, joy, power, and excellence. He is looking deep into our past and healing us of all the mental and emotional pain we have experienced in our life so far. There are so many amazing things that are happening throughout our body, soul, and spirit throughout this process that we aren't even aware of. Do not try to keep track of everything He is doing or figure it all out. Just remember since God created you, He knows how to completely restore you to even better than original condition. This is because in addition to healing you and filling you with His goodness, He is also fully training and equipping you for your calling and destiny. After this season of transformation, you will have gifts, talents, abilities, and even personality traits you never had before. Like a professionally trained Olympic athlete, God is making sure you are fully prepared and ready to run the race He is calling you to.

So how long must we wait? Depending on what a person has been through and what God is calling them to, this season could range from a few months to several years. The good news is, when God has us in a season of transformation, He still works through us and allows us to function in our area of gifting and destiny to some degree. Then, once the necessary transformation is complete, He releases us into the season where He allows us to be used on a continual basis in the fullness of our calling and destiny.

One final thought on waiting and the importance of it. A woman who becomes pregnant begins to feel and experience things she never has before. One feeling virtually every woman experiences during pregnancy is being uncomfortable; and the longer she is pregnant, the more uncomfortable she becomes. But any good mother wants her baby to be full term so he or she will be born healthy and strong. We need to remind ourselves that although we may be uncomfortable, we want our "baby", (which is God's dream and destiny for our life), to be fully developed, healthy, and strong so it can thrive and be a blessing to the surrounding world in which it lives.

Day 19 Prayer of a Champion

"God, I'm so grateful You want me to be fully healed, empowered, and equipped when You finally release me into the fullness of my calling and destiny. Give me the courage to go when you say, "Go", and the patience to wait when you say, "Wait". I know Your wisdom regarding the direction of my life is supreme and Your timing is perfect. Cause me to humbly walk beside You and continually learn from You until You release me. I thank You that the longer I wait, the stronger You are making me. I give You permission to further cleanse, fill, empower, and equip me as I continue to wait on You. I am comforted in knowing my waiting will enable me to bear much fruit and thrive in my calling and destiny. As I live each day, help me to stay close to You and patient as Your dream and destiny for my life continue to fully develop. Amen!"

Day 20

Loyalty and Faithfulness

~

"Everyone talks about how loyal and faithful he is, but just try to find someone who really is!"

Proverbs 20:6 GNT

It is good for us to express our loyalty and faithfulness with words, but it is even better to express them with our ongoing work ethic, habits, and deeds. It seems in today's world, loyalty and faithfulness to family, friends, a geographic location, or a particular company as an employee is becoming more and more a thing of the past. Loyalty and faithfulness, however, make up a large foundation block upon which strong families, friendships, communities, and companies are built.

I realize seasons change and people move on to other places and things, but many people are uprooting and changing their place in life simply because they were offended, hurt, or do not like a decision that was made. This response and pattern of behavior, however, ends up damaging us in both the short and long term.

The beautiful thing about God is He models so much loyalty and faithfulness for us since He and His

Word do not change. Nothing we could ever do would cause Him to love us less or leave us. We cannot earn His love or His salvation – they are simply a gift we must humbly receive. Once we choose to follow God wholeheartedly, we are safe in His arms and we can expect to live with Him forever in Heaven. This beautiful picture of loyalty and faithfulness from God to us should translate into how loyal and faithful we are to the people around us.

The key to following this principle throughout our lives is to not dwell on how loyal and faithful others are to us. We cannot control whether people like us or whether they will be loyal and faithful to us, but we can control how loyal and faithful we will be to others. We can accomplish this and stay strong by reminding ourselves of how loyal and faithful God is, and then do our best each day to model our life and behavior after His example.

On a practical level, this means we should do everything we can on a daily basis to support our boss and the company we work for and represent. We may not agree with every policy and decision our boss or company makes, but since as a company we are all on the same team, we should wear the "uniform" with pride and score as many "points" for our team as possible. Unlike some who change their job every time they don't agree with their boss or company, we should honor and work for our boss with respect, diligence, and excellence for as long as God has us in that season. Decide in your mind when you go into work each day that you are going to be loyal and faithful to your boss and your company for as long as God has you there. As you do this each day, God will bless and reward you for honoring Him and His Word in your daily life.

Our loyalty and faithfulness is determined not only by what we do, but also by what we say. Who we speak of and how we speak about them also reveals a lot about our loyalty and faithfulness. We should decide that throughout our life we will not be a person who starts, listens to, or spreads gossip. Let's be very conscious of our words and make sure we are speaking well of people both when they are with us and when they are not. Being truly loyal and faithful means we are loyal and faithful in every area – our thoughts, words, and actions; 24 hours a day, 7 days a week. We are loyal and faithful because God is and we are both His child and representative. Because of this, nothing and no one should alter our level of loyalty and faithfulness.

In light of everything we have discussed today, there are of course certainly going to be times when we should constructively analyze and criticize certain decisions and policies, but it must be done with the people who actually have the power to make a change. It should also be said that our contribution to the conversation should not originate from a heart of pride or selfish motives but rather of love and concern for the person or organization we are talking about. The end result of anything we say about a person or organization should be for their improvement and progression forward.

We will have a clearer conscience and sleep better at night knowing we do everything in our power throughout the day to be loyal, faithful, and to only speak well of others – even when they are not in our presence. Let's choose to be people of deep love, honor, and respect. For this will surely bring a smile to God's face and cause Him to be pleased and very proud of us at the end of each day.

~

Day 20 Prayer of a Champion

"God, cause me to highly value loyalty and faithfulness in my life and in the choices I make. I am so grateful You are the epitome of loyalty and faithfulness. My life, salvation, and eternity with You are safe and secure because of Your great loyalty and faithfulness to me. Help me to honor my superiors, my school, and my company by being loyal and faithful to them for as long as You have me there. May I never participate in or entertain gossip, and cause me to always speak well of others even when they are not around. Empower me to always be constructive with my words and may I always seek to improve the people I interact with and the organizations I am a part of. Amen!"

DAY 21

ONGOING EVALUATION, MAINTENANCE, AND IMPROVEMENT

~

"GOOD PEOPLE THINK CAREFULLY ABOUT WHAT THEY DO."

PROVERBS 21:29 NCV

The saying, "If it isn't broken, don't fix it" is not a very wise policy for how we should handle people or things in life. For many things, if they are not maintained, they will eventually break; and we all know it is easier and less expensive to maintain something than to fix or replace it. This is true for our personal and professional lives as well. If we want to stay sharp, healthy, and continually advance forward through life, we must be willing and ready to continually learn, grow, and remain flexible for the ever changing environments and circumstances of both life and business.

We cannot turn a blind eye to our daily routines and habits and think everything is going to be fine. Nor can we lead a family, run a business, or work for a company and never evaluate the overall health and performance of ourselves, other employees or family members, and the organization or family as a whole. Remember, we should not be trying to simply plateau and survive through life. God wants us to be continually improving and thriving in every area of our lives. What worked for us last year probably won't work for us this year if we expect to become increasingly more efficient and productive throughout the duration of our lives.

For example, if you have recently been promoted, then you know your boss will most likely expect more responsibility, leadership, effort, and productivity from you than when you were serving in your previous role. This increasing level of leadership and productivity should not only be expected of us at work, but in every area of our lives. We should be continually evaluating and improving as a parent, friend, son or daughter, spouse, athlete, employee, and simply as a fellow citizen of the earth. We are all members of the human family and so it is our responsibility to do our best to help the earth become increasingly more safe, clean, loving, and kind.

On a personal note, we should ask ourselves occasionally, "Am I more loving, patient, and kind than I was a year ago?" Are we still struggling with the same bad habits or have we overcome at least one or some of them? And finally, are we taking better care of our bodies by eating healthier, exercising, and getting an adequate amount of sleep each night? Since our lives are so precious and short, we must be vigilant and intentional when it comes to ongoing personal evaluation, maintenance, and improvement.

As we have mentioned before, our best days should always be in front of us. Our lives, then, if drawn out on graph paper, should be progressing in a steady line that is continually moving forward and upward. The only way this will be true is if we closely walk with the Lord, continually listen to what He is saying, and do our best to apply what He says to our everyday lives.

Have you ever driven through a developing neighborhood where new houses were being built? Most likely you noticed some of the houses were just a foundation, some had a foundation plus the wood or steel framing, and some were completely finished with all the decorative trim and a fresh coat of paint. When a contractor builds one of these beautifully ornate homes, he has the blueprints and he works on the home a little each day. He knows what the finished project will look like, but he first starts with the foundation and then eventually completes the home with decorative trim work.

So it is with God and our lives. When we start a personal relationship with Him, He begins to build us up in our new identity as His son or daughter. He begins with the large foundational issues that must be established in our lives and then He slowly builds us up until we are spiritually mature and complete in Him. God brings us through this process to strengthen us, transform us to be more like Him, and to empower us to shine bright to the world around us.

When it comes to being God's child, do not settle for being just a foundation or a foundation with only the wood or steel framing completed. Allow God to build and install the rooms, hallways, staircases, windows, roof, and even the decorative trim so you will be a complete, strong, and masterfully crafted house where His life and presence can dwell. And since God calls us to continually improve throughout the duration of our lives, always seek to perfect your "house" by both maintaining what He has already built, and by adding items and decorations to your home that will make it even more inviting, useful, and beautiful.

~

Day 21 Prayer of a Champion

"Help me God to think carefully about my actions and to be proactive about my life and relationships. May I always seek to improve who I am and the relationships I have. I always want to be moving forward and so show me which bad habits I should work on right now in my life. I long to live at my best and so reveal to me what adjustments I need to make in order to be living a full and productive life that is pleasing to You. Please build a strong foundation in my life and then fully construct me into the beautiful "home" You have created me to be. Thank You for seeing the best in me and continually leading me forward and upward to reaching my greatest potential. Amen!"

DAY 22

SKILL AND EXCELLENCE

~

**"DO YOU SEE PEOPLE SKILLED IN THEIR WORK? THEY
WILL WORK FOR KINGS, NOT FOR ORDINARY PEOPLE."**

PROVERBS 22:29 NCV

One time I was asked to perform the invocation and
benediction for an Eagle Scout Court of Honor
ceremony. Considering how few Boy Scouts earn this
distinguished rank and achievement, I was quite
honored to be a part of this special ceremony. As I
prayed about what I would say and what verse I would
share, I felt led to share the verse we are discussing
today – Proverbs 22:29. As you can imagine, if a young
man wishes to earn the rank of Eagle Scout, he must be
an individual with great dedication, persistence, skill,
and excellence. This verse, then, is very fitting for this
outstanding achievement since it speaks of individuals
who have distinguished themselves from the crowd
and become so amazing at what they do that they even
earn the respect of world leaders.

Feeling confident this was a good verse to share at
the ceremony, I drove to the venue where it was being

hosted and walked inside to meet the family. After introducing myself and offering my congratulations, I noticed a table with photos and scrapbooks filled with memorabilia of this young man's life leading up to this monumental day. One scrapbook in particular really impressed me. It was full of photos and letters from key social, religious, political, and military leaders from all over the world. I could hardly believe it. Here is a young man who hasn't even completed high school and yet he has earned the recognition and respect of renowned leaders from all around the world. Simply amazing! A young man sets out to complete a certain number of achievements in a certain allotment of time and then receives the recognition and respect of world leaders because of his accomplishment. This made me wonder – how much could we all learn from this young man's character, focus, and discipline?

Although it is true most of us will never be an Eagle Scout, everyone in life does in fact go through a type of rank and advancement process. And just like with Boy Scouts, our pace and level of advancement depends upon our character, focus, discipline, dedication, skill, and excellence. Every day we face a variety of tests and challenges. How we handle these tests and challenges determines whether we are moving on to the next achievement, or whether we will have to try and pass that test again in the future.

Excellence and going the extra mile are always worth the extra effort. Decide today you are not going to live your life in a way that simply allows you to do as little as possible to get by. Choose to do things well and with excellence; knowing you represent a beautiful and awesome God who created and sustains the entire universe. We will never be perfect, but we can do our best each day and be both professional and excellent in all we do. For we are all carrying the baton in our generation which was passed down to us from excellent and amazing men and women who lived before us.

I challenge us to take a good look at the big picture of our lives and ask ourselves, do we want to spend our lives pecking at the ground like ordinary birds, or do we want to spend our lives soaring through the sky like eagles? If we want to feel the wind on our face, see the glory of the sun rising and setting, and soar with other eagles, then we are going to have to do what it takes to live, think, speak, and act like an eagle.

Day 22 Prayer of a Champion

"Cause me God to distinguish myself from the crowd and become the person of character, focus, and discipline You have created me to be. Because I live to please and represent You, I wish to achieve the highest "rank" possible during my time on the earth and so help me to successfully advance through all of the tests and challenges I will face. Give me the strength and tenacity to always do my best and to go the extra mile even when others will not. Empower me to carry the baton in my generation with great excellence, skill, and honor so I can one day pass it on to the next generation of leaders. Cause me to dream big and to live and work in such a way that I am able to soar with other eagles throughout my life. Amen!"

DAY 23

MENTAL, EMOTIONAL, AND SPIRITUAL STABILITY

~

"LET REVERENCE FOR THE LORD BE THE CONCERN OF YOUR LIFE."

PROVERBS 23:17 GNT

~

"BE WISE, AND DIRECT YOUR MIND IN THE WAY [OF THE LORD]."

PROVERBS 23:19 AMP

We do not have to believe or act upon everything we think. Thoughts come into our minds throughout the day and we must carefully decide whether we will allow them to seep into our hearts or if we will immediately dismiss them and override them with the truth of God's Word. For sure, there is so much happening around us and even to us at any given moment. Because of this, it is certainly understandable why people struggle with issues like fear, anxiety, insecurity, and depression. Today, I would like to encourage us to keep our minds focused on the Lord and what He says about us no matter what is happening around us or to us.

What it really boils down to and what my prayer for us is we would be able to consistently live in a place where the thoughts, opinions, praise, criticism, acceptance, and rejection of others do not alter our spiritual, mental, and emotional state. As His child and friend, God wants us to be unmovable and unshakeable; steady and strong in His arms and presence.

When our thoughts and concerns are on God and what is happening in His Kingdom, the negative things that are happening in the world and in our everyday lives will seem much less powerful and significant. So many people allow the news as well as the thoughts and words of others control their levels of peace, joy, and confidence. God, however, wants our levels of peace, joy, and confidence to only be affected and controlled by who He is and what He says about us. When this becomes true in our everyday lives, we will no longer walk in timidity and insecurity. For when God's opinion of us becomes the only one that matters, that is when we will walk in unprecedented freedom, confidence, and boldness.

So how do we do this? We must know the mind and heart of God, what His Word says concerning the world around us, and who we are as His child. When we fill our minds and hearts with His Word, its influence and "volume" in our lives will become much stronger and louder than the defeating and crippling thoughts that once kept us bound.

God wants you to be mighty, effective, and productive in both the geographical location and area of expertise He has you in. He wants you to be so spiritually, mentally, and emotionally strong that you are able to be strong and stable enough for yourself, while also being strong and stable enough to help others. The only way this is possible is if we continually stay close to God's heart, His Word, and His presence. When these intangible ingredients become a regular part of our daily habits and routine, we will see tangible benefits and rewards in our life, home, workplace, church, and community.

Regardless of what is happening to you, around you, or in the world, decide you are going to fully believe and trust what God and His Word say concerning you and the world around you. And since the aim is to live strong and healthy lives marked by spiritual, mental, and emotional stability, let's also choose each day to stay consistently peaceful, joyful, and confident.

Day 23 Prayer of a Champion

"God, teach me to carefully filter my thoughts through who You are and what Your Word says. Keep me from feeling pressured to believe or act upon everything that comes into my mind. Empower me to remain balanced and stable throughout the day in my spirit, mind, and emotions. Teach me to live in such a way that my levels of peace, joy, and confidence are only affected by who You are and what You say about me. I pray the influence and the volume of Your Word will be stronger and louder than any other thoughts I have throughout the day. I thank You that when I live this way, You promise to keep me in a consistent place of peace, joy, confidence, and stability. Amen!"

Day 24

Never Give Up

~

"No matter how often honest people fall, they always get up again."

Proverbs 24:16 GNT

As a young boy and teenager growing up, I always thought the people who became successful accomplished their dreams on their first try with no setbacks or failures along the way. Then in my twenties, when I began studying the lives of world leaders and successful individuals, I realized many of the people who we admire as being the best in their field throughout history had some major obstacles and setbacks they had to overcome in order to reach the level of success they are renowned for.

We all were created to accomplish something remarkable before we die. We may not achieve all of our personal goals and dreams, but if we seek the Lord for His wisdom, guidance, and provision, then we will certainly achieve every goal and dream He has destined us to accomplish. And let me remind you that His goals and dreams for us are always more incredible, satisfying, and fulfilling than our own personal goals and dreams.

On the days when it seems like God has forgotten about us or is no longer concerned with the success of our dreams, we have to continually remind ourselves that God has an amazing plan for our lives, He wants us to succeed, and He wants us flourishing and thriving in both who we are as His child, and in what we were created to accomplish for Him.

Some people experience multiple failures before they finally see breakthrough and achieve success. If this is also true for us, then we will have to decide – will failure generate discouragement and depression in us and stop us from moving forward, or will we allow failure to be one of the things that challenges us to become better and try again? Since today we are talking about never giving up, I pray failure will only generate more hope and even greater passion in you so you will keep moving forward until you ultimately succeed and fulfill God's destiny for your life.

God does not and cannot fail. If we are living for Him, working with Him, and staying close to Him, He will reveal to us what adjustments need to be made in order for us to overcome the setback or obstacle we are facing, so we can be one step closer to fulfilling our destiny.

As we have learned, everybody falls – but not everybody gets back up. Choose to get back up; again, and again, and again. Stay enthusiastic and be determined to fulfill your destiny. Life is so short and we only get one shot at it. I know one thing that will not be fun for any of us is looking back on our lives when we are 60 or 70 years old and wondering who we could have been, and what we could have accomplished if we had not given up. May we never even have the opportunity to do this because we have purposed in our heart to stay the course and follow after God and His plan for us no matter what!

~

Day 24 Prayer of a Champion

"God, help me to remember failure is inevitable along the road to success. Cause me to always see failure as another chance to learn, grow, and move one step closer toward my destiny. I'm so grateful You are on my side and that You want me to succeed. May I seek Your guidance and help each day as I pursue the dreams You have destined me to achieve. Take away any unhealthy fear of failing and instead fill me with Your tenacity and courage so I will always get up and continue to move forward no matter what. Amen!"

DAY 25

BEAUTIFUL, PRECIOUS, AND HIGHLY VALUABLE

~

"TAKE THE IMPURITIES OUT OF SILVER AND THE ARTIST CAN PRODUCE A THING OF BEAUTY."

PROVERBS 25:4 GNT

Silver and gold – they are beautiful, precious, and highly valuable. People dig deep into the earth to find them, and then other people take the time to purify them so their greatest potential and worth can be revealed. This process is also true for us. Inside of us, deep down under the surface of what most people see and hear of us on a daily basis, lies precious gifts, talents, and the potential God placed inside of us before we were even born.

First we discover God, acknowledge His existence and supremacy in both the universe and our lives, and then we invite Him to save us and lead us through this life and eventually into all eternity with Him. After acknowledging God's supremacy and beginning a relationship with Him, the next step in our Christian journey should be for us to give God full access into all we are, and all we have. When we do this, God then reaches in and extracts all of the gifts, talents, and potential He Himself so graciously and generously instilled into us.

We were never meant to live ordinary, plain lives. If we do end up living a plain and ordinary life, it is simply because we did not allow God to peel back and uncover who we truly are as His child. Surely we can be any number of things; countless titles and career paths exist all around the world, and we can try to fit into any one of them. But we were created for something more. God has a Kingdom title and career path that belongs to you and you alone. It is this specific high calling He wants you to pursue and function in during your time on the earth.

In order for this to happen, we must first be prepared by the artist and made beautiful by His design and skill. With silver and gold, they are heated to extreme temperatures and all of the impurities eventually rise to the top. These impurities are then removed so only the silver and gold in its purest form remain. So in our lives, when we feel like things are hot, uncomfortable, and even painful, God is simply removing the impurities and making you more beautiful, precious, and valuable. With this in mind, our comfort can be found in knowing that the fewer impurities we have, the more beautiful, precious, and valuable we will be.

Since God does not use literal fire to purify us, how does He remove the impurities from our lives? I believe He uses His Word, His presence, and even the people and the everyday circumstances of our lives to melt off the things that are holding us back and keeping us from reaching our highest potential and greatest worth. Like I mentioned, this can be uncomfortable and even painful, but we must keep the end result in mind.

Comparing our lives to silver and gold metaphorically, a piece of silver or gold resting deep within the earth probably does not like getting blasted by dynamite or chipped away at by machines. It probably does not like getting shipped all around the world and placed in a furnace where its very essence is separated and rearranged. The entire time this is all happening, the silver or gold is probably wishing it was left alone in the earth to simply be. But what is the end result? Once the silver or gold is ready, it is placed in a shiny display case with other very beautiful, precious, and highly valuable items that went through the same process. Items of silver and gold are also carefully selected to be used by the finest people for the finest occasions in all the world. They are cherished and admired by their owners as well as those who see them.

With all of this in mind, let's not complain or want to be left alone when things get uncomfortable. Instead, let's stay focused on the end result and continue to remind ourselves that God is the artist. He is simply purifying us so we will become more beautiful, precious, and highly valuable – which eventually will lead to us attaining our greatest potential and worth.

Day 25 Prayer of a Champion

"God, I'm so grateful You have placed within me tremendous potential and talents, and that I am a person of priceless worth. It amazes me that even though You are the God of the entire universe, I am precious in Your sight and You highly value me as Your child. I make myself available to You by giving You access to the gifts You have placed inside of me. I ask You to extract them one by one and use them to glorify Yourself and help others. Cause me to discover and live out the Kingdom title and career path You have ordained for me. When things get "hot" and uncomfortable in my life, help me to remember You are simply purifying me so I can become even more beautiful, precious, and valuable. I know You have an amazing plan and purpose for me and so help me to embrace the journey and the process of being refined. You know what is best for me and I trust You are getting me ready to do extraordinary things. Amen!"

DAY 26

SPEAK LIFE

~

"SOMEONE WHO MISLEADS SOMEONE ELSE AND THEN CLAIMS THAT HE WAS ONLY JOKING IS LIKE A MAD PERSON PLAYING WITH A DEADLY WEAPON."

PROVERBS 26:18-19 GNT

We all want to enjoy life, have fun, and laugh with our family and friends. But creating or being in an environment of constant sarcasm and coarse joking can quickly become very exhausting and draining. When we step back and look at the brevity of life and the one chance we receive to make a positive and eternal difference on the earth, is this really the kind of atmosphere we want to create or be a part of most of the time? After traveling to different parts of America and the world over the years, it seems to me the world is already full of enough deception, negativity, and sarcasm without us adding to it.

Of course none of us are perfect and at times we are going to say things we are not proud of. The point of today's lesson, though, is to encourage us to be aligned a little closer with the heart of God and be more careful and intentional about the words we say.

I believe God would be pleased if we did our best each day to live in between being so serious and boring that no one wants to be around us, and being so sarcastic, cruel, and obnoxious that we end up leaving hurt people and a trail of mess everywhere we go. Somewhere in the middle of these two extremes is a playful, friendly, and encouraging person whose words and actions make God proud and bring a smile to His face. This is the type of person we should aim to be.

Many people are walking around each day with poor self-esteem, feelings of inadequacy, and even depression. This is why it is so vital we do everything in our power to speak life and contribute to the positive words that are being said throughout the world. On a practical level, if you know someone and their situation and you have something loving, kind, or encouraging to say to them, then you should tell them. As long as it comes from a pure heart of love, then that person will most likely be very grateful you courageously took the time and effort to brighten their day. On the extreme level, your words of encouragement and hope may even prevent someone from doing something dangerous or harmful to themselves or someone else. With this sobering truth in mind, let's not walk around with amazing and beautiful words in our hearts and minds that could be and should be shared with those who need to hear them.

Wouldn't it be awesome if one day you found out someone didn't give up on their dreams or on life simply because of what you said to them? Never underestimate the power of your words or your ability to inspire someone to be better.

This principle of being careful with our words and speaking life applies to what we say to ourselves as well. Some of us may not even realize it, but if you pay close attention throughout the day, you may hear yourself saying negative, hurtful, and defeating things about yourself and your future. Just some of the negative things people say about themselves are that they are unattractive, overweight, not good enough for someone or something, and unfortunately many other damaging things.

What we must come to realize and understand is our words are not just sound that dissipates into the air. Words are powerful and they have a strong effect on those who hear them. The Bible says our words help to steer the course of our lives as well as the lives of those we speak to (See James 3:1-12). Considering this principle and the words we say to ourselves and to others, in which direction are we steering our own lives and the lives of those we speak to? Are we steering ourselves and others toward discouragement, belittlement, and defeat; or are we steering ourselves and others toward a better and greater place than where we currently are – a place of encouragement, empowerment, and success?

Whether we realize it or not, the words we speak are being recorded by ourselves, those who hear us, and even by God in Heaven. What will the recording sound like at the end of our lives? Let's not arrive in

Heaven and be ashamed of what we said to ourselves and others. By carefully and intentionally choosing our words throughout each day, we can stand before God when we arrive in Heaven both satisfied and confident; knowing we spoke life, hope, and encouragement at every opportunity possible over ourselves and the people we came in contact with.

~

Day 26 Prayer of a Champion

"God, I'm so grateful You are the author of life and that You speak life over me and over everyone You created. Instead of sarcasm and coarse joking, cause me to make the most of my life and my words by staying positive and promoting an atmosphere of encouragement and love everywhere I go. I recognize my words are powerful and so teach me to align my words with Your heart and to speak words of life over myself and those around me. I never know what others are really going through and so empower me to always be kind and positive with my words. I also wish to encourage and build others up so help me to be very careful and intentional with what I say. I wish to move forward and help others rise higher so cause me to speak the inspiring words that will ultimately steer both myself and others toward a greater place of encouragement, empowerment, and success. Amen!"

DAY 27

HUMILITY

~

"DON'T BRAG ABOUT TOMORROW! EACH DAY BRINGS ITS OWN SURPRISES. DON'T BRAG ABOUT YOURSELF – LET OTHERS PRAISE YOU."

PROVERBS 27:1-2 CEV

Life is so short, precious, and unpredictable. No matter how experienced we become, life will always be a fragile thing that none of us can truly predict from day to day.

Our strength, health, and ability to be successful in what we do ultimately originate with and depend on God. Even breathing and getting out of bed in the morning require His strength and grace in our lives. In addition, no matter what we accomplish throughout our lifetime, we should always acknowledge it was because of God and the gifts He so graciously gave us that we were able to achieve our successes.

Humility also functions as a foundation for many other positive virtues. For example, kindness, compassion, and respect all rest on the foundation of humility. Since we were all created equally by God, we should respect all people the same. Unfortunately, some people offer respect to others based on their age, social status, or title. This is not wise. God graciously created each one of us in His image and we are all here together on the earth under His guidance, protection, and care. You may have heard it said that we are no better than anyone, and we are also no worse than anyone. We should simply be content in who God created us to be without being intimidated by or looking down on anybody else.

God loves humility and the sobering reality is God actually stands against proud people, but He helps those who are humble (See James 4:6). With this in mind, we certainly do not want the all–powerful and all–knowing God of the universe opposing us or our efforts in life. No matter how smart, wealthy, or successful we become, we will always need His guidance, direction, and favor throughout the duration of our lives.

Humility is the virtue that allows us to stay soft, moldable, and able to change. Things and people that are healthy and strong grow and change throughout their lifetime. For example, just think of all the changes plants and trees go through in order to grow and stay healthy. Without humility, we will eventually become arrogant, self–sufficient, and rigid; unable to hear God's whisper or the loving and wise counsel of family, friends, and colleagues.

So in light of what we've discussed today, let's continue to remind ourselves that everything we are, and everything we have, comes from God. He is the One who supplies us with the strength and the ability to attain and enjoy the things we have. As we intentionally walk in humility each day, we will stay in a place where God can continually protect, help, and bless us. And since we are all on this earth together, humility will also enable us to walk with fellow humans in a place of mutual love, honor, and respect.

~

Day 27 Prayer of a Champion

"Cause me to always walk closely with you God with a heart of humility. I recognize all my gifts, talents, and even the air I breathe come from You. Help me to maintain a tender heart of humility so I will consistently treat others with a deep sense of kindness, compassion, and respect. I recognize no matter how knowledgeable or successful I become, I will always need Your wisdom, guidance, and favor in my life. Throughout my lifetime, enable me to stay humble and teachable so I can change, grow, and be healthy through the many seasons of life. Amen!"

DAY 28

JOY, CELEBRATION, AND GRATITUDE

~

"BLESSED (HAPPY, FORTUNATE, AND TO BE ENVIED) IS THE MAN WHO REVERENTLY AND WORSHIPFULLY FEARS [THE LORD] AT ALL TIMES [REGARDLESS OF CIRCUMSTANCES]."

PROVERBS 28:14 AMP

We were created to enjoy a healthy and vibrant relationship with God both throughout each day and throughout our lives. God is our Heavenly Father and He promises to always take care of us and even give us more than enough so we can also help take care of others. If we will simply look up and acknowledge His existence, love, and provision in our lives, we will see and realize that He shines upon us and provides for us each and every day.

The world, its people, and life in general are beautiful and fascinating. May we never lose our sense of awe and wonder regarding how awesome God is. We are not here to simply endure life, but to enjoy life. Even if it seems like the farthest thing from our daily reality right now, life is meant to be a glorious adventure where we continue to grow in both awareness and appreciation regarding God, people, the things we have, and the things we experience.

The Bible says in God's presence is fullness of joy (See Psalm 16:11). As we acknowledge, thank, and praise Him for who He is and what He does, our joy will both increase and remain consistent throughout the ups and downs of daily living.

By focusing on the good and the blessings in our lives, and by keeping our mind and eyes always on God, we will find ourselves living in a continual state of spiritual, mental, and emotional stability. Don't allow the enemy and his lies to confuse you or rob you of your peace and joy. When we spend our time being grateful and thanking God for what He has done for us and given to us, we will have little time left over to complain, feel sorry for ourselves, or think about what we do not have.

Just like today's verse says, regardless of our circumstances, let's worship and have reverence for the Lord with an attitude and disposition of joy, celebration, and gratitude. God already knows what we need and He already knows how He will meet that need long before we even think to ask Him for help. Life is too short to be worrying, wishing, or feeling sorry for ourselves. Choose joy, choose to celebrate, choose to be thankful, and choose to make your life one long worship song to the God who gives us life and everything else we will ever need.

Day 28 Prayer of a Champion

"You are amazing God. I'm so grateful my greatest calling in life is to simply have a healthy and vibrant relationship with You. Above all, You want me to enjoy spending time with You on a daily basis. I acknowledge your existence, love, and provision in my life and I thank You that You will always take care of me and even give me more than enough. Teach me to approach each day with a sense of appreciation and joy; knowing the world and its people are fascinating and amazing. Because of this, may I enjoy life and be both excited and grateful for all the amazing opportunities and blessings each day brings. Empower me to keep my mind and my eyes always on You so I can live in a consistent state of spiritual, mental, and emotional peace. Amen!"

Day 29

Hope and Expectations

~

"Everybody wants the good will of the ruler, but only from the Lord can you get justice."

Proverbs 29:26 GNT

As we go through life, there are certain necessities we all need for the journey. For example, some basic needs we all require as humans are to be loved, protected, and taken care of. But where should we expect these things to come from? It's easy to say our family, friends, and even our job; but true and lasting safety, security, and provision ultimately come from God alone. He is the original source of all life, provision, and blessing.

It is easy to put our hope and expectation in people because we can see both them and what they materially have. Even though God owns everything and has more than enough for us, it is more difficult to trust Him at times because we cannot physically see Him nor can we see where the security and provision will come from. When we view situations through the eyes of our spirit, however, it is plain to see God is truly the only

One who can be trusted and counted on forever and for everything.

One translation of this verse actually talks about *waiting* for God's justice. This is key because the Bible says those who wait on the Lord will actually become stronger (See Isaiah 40:31). I believe waiting on the Lord makes us stronger because while we wait, our eyes shift more and more off of what people can do for us and we begin to place our hope and expectation only on God and what He can do for us.

Of course, most of the time God works through people to deliver His provision and blessings to us, but the heart of the matter is where our focus, hope, and expectation lie while we are waiting. When we place our hope in people, we are only setting ourselves up for disillusionment. Disillusionment is an ugly thing and it is not something we want to intentionally bring into our lives – it causes disappointment, frustration, and even anger. When we trust in God alone to provide for us and take care of us, we avoid this nasty pitfall.

The Bible says an individual who trusts in people is like a dead, dried up bush or tumbleweed in the desert while those who trust in God are like fruitful trees planted by the river with lush, green leaves (See Jeremiah 17:5-8). You don't have to think about that comparison for too long; all of us would obviously prefer to be a lush, fruitful tree by the river instead of a dead, dried up bush or tumbleweed.

There was a particular time in my life when I left a job in sales making close to $50,000 a year to help my friend pastor his church for $50 a week. We moved our whole family to a new state and trusted if God was calling us to do this, then He would take care of us. Shortly after moving to our new location and beginning to help my friend in ministry, we could not find a job to supplement our income but checks began to show up in our mailbox without us even telling anyone what we were doing, or what our needs were. This was obviously a huge faith building experience for us and very reassuring. A few months later, we pondered the idea of writing financial support letters to family and friends. Since God was miraculously sending checks in the mail, we wondered if we should start asking for monthly financial support or simply trust that the Lord would continue to miraculously provide. As I wrestled with this decision, I asked God to speak to me and confirm to me what He wanted us to do. I was reading in Psalms one day and the following verse was a clear sign and revelation from the Lord. It read, "It is better to trust in the LORD than to depend on human beings" (Psalm 118:8 GNB). Wow! Ok God, I guess I know what you're trying to tell me! God does use monthly financial support and at other times He supernaturally provides without us even asking. In this particular season, He was teaching us to wholeheartedly trust Him without making our needs known to people.

One comforting way to look at all of this is, if we don't have it, then we don't need it or God is not ready to give it to us yet. Trust that what you have is what you need and that God is not holding anything good from you. He wants to bless you and do amazing things in your life even more than you do. So relax and seek

Him and remind yourself He will give to you and work through you when the time is right and you are ready.

After reading today's teaching, I hope it is plain to see God is big enough and powerful enough to provide everything we will ever need – love, protection, defense, vindication, and provision. Let's spend our lives looking to God with hopeful expectation; knowing He deeply loves us and delights in taking good care of us. He alone is our source and as we put our trust in Him, we will be like strong, lush trees by the river that are always flourishing, thriving, and fruitful.

~

Day 29 Prayer of a Champion

"God, I'm so grateful You are my source and that my security and provision ultimately come from You. Although I cannot see You with my natural eyes, teach me to trust You and look at my needs through the eyes of my spirit. I know You love me and You have everything I will ever need. Even when I have to wait, I know You are making me stronger and causing my focus to shift off of people and onto You. I do not want to fall into the pit of disillusionment and disappointment so empower me to put my hope and expectation only in You. Help me to relax and to always know I have exactly what I need for today. Thank You for always being such a wonderful Father to me. Amen!"

Day 30

God is in Control

~

"Don't blow the whistle on your fellow workers behind their backs; they'll accuse you of being underhanded, and then you'll be the guilty one!"

Proverbs 30:10 MSG

For those unfamiliar with the terms "blow the whistle" or "whistle–blower", it basically means to report a person's bad behavior to an individual in higher authority. Throughout life, we are all going to experience unfair treatment and injustice to both us and to those around us. Today's teaching will help you learn how to properly handle these situations in a way that pleases God, protects you from getting wrapped up in the drama, and assures your ongoing success and blessing in life.

Unfortunately not everyone you live with, go to school with, or work with is aiming to be a champion in life. Some people are willing to compromise what they know is right in order to get ahead; even if it means taking advantage of organizations and people in the process.

So what do we do when someone like this is in our daily life and we know what they are doing? I have discovered through studying the Bible and trial and error that in most cases, the best policy is to mind our own business, work hard, and do the best we can. After all, we cannot control anybody else or force them to change. People are going to make their own decisions and so all we can do is love people, pray for them, and model good behavior.

It should be said here that obviously this principle does not apply when someone's life is in danger. If we know information that could potentially save someone's life because of abuse, illegal drugs, or self-harm, then it is our civil and moral obligation to speak up and help a fellow human being who is in imminent danger.

For the majority of the time when a person's life is not in danger, we should remind ourselves God is in control of both our lives and our circumstances. Someone who is behaving inappropriately in your life directly or around you will eventually be found out and their actions and words will be dealt with accordingly. By us exposing a person and trying to be a hero really only jeopardizes us getting wrapped up in the mess of the drama – which could easily lead to us getting in trouble as well and having our reputation tainted in the process.

God is neither blind nor deaf to us or the situations we face in life. He sees you, your family, your school, and your workplace. When it seems like God is a million miles away with His back turned away from you and what is happening in your life, you must remind yourself God sees everything and He promises to defend, vindicate, and bring justice to your situation.

God always gets the final word. Think of life and our circumstances like a giant chess game where it is God versus the Devil and our enemies. No matter how much it looks like the Devil and/or our enemies are winning, God always gets the final move of the game – plus He always wins. Trust that God is in control of your circumstances and that His love will not allow you to experience something you cannot handle.

So be encouraged today. You don't have to control or change anyone nor do you have to be a superhero. God is in control and He cares about you as well as the seemingly insignificant details of your everyday circumstances. Choose to believe today and every day that no matter what is happening to you or around you that God is with you, for you, and He is going to use everything that is happening for your good and His glory. As you live out these principles on a daily basis, simply do your best to work hard, stay positive, and be the champion God has created you to be.

Day 30 Prayer of a Champion

"God, I'm so grateful You see everything and You are ultimately in control. Help me to avoid the trap of being a whistle blower when I see or personally experience injustice. Since I cannot control people or situations, empower me to simply do what I know is right and be the best I can on a daily basis. Since You are the only One who can truly change an individual, cause me to simply love others, pray for them, and model good behavior to those around me. I know You are aware and in ultimate control of what is happening to me and so I trust You will protect, defend, and vindicate me. I'm so grateful You will never allow me to experience something I cannot handle and that Your great love always wins. Empower me to stay positive and to be the champion You have created me to be. Amen!"

DAY 31

AIM HIGH

~

"A TRULY GOOD WIFE IS THE MOST PRECIOUS TREASURE A MAN CAN FIND! WITH GREAT PRIDE HER HUSBAND SAYS, 'THERE ARE MANY GOOD WOMEN, BUT YOU ARE THE BEST!'"

PROVERBS 31:10, 28 CEV

Although this chapter of Proverbs speaks mostly of a noble wife and mother, including some of her praiseworthy actions and accomplishments, I believe the principles throughout the chapter are applicable to anyone who wants to live the life of a champion. This chapter is also a perfect one to conclude our devotional with since it speaks of character and excellence permeating every area of one's life and daily routine. By reading, studying, and applying the truths in Proverbs 31, we will grow a little each day into the champion God has created us to be.

The husband in the above verses carefully chose an outstanding woman to be both his lifetime partner and the mother who would eventually birth and raise his children. By reading the rest of the chapter, we can also see the man and woman in this chapter not only picked a great spouse, but they both also chose great routines, habits, relationships, and ways to make a living.

What I want to encourage and challenge all of us to do today and from this day forward is to aim high. In addition to an amazing spouse that will be a fantastic match just for you, there are amazing habits, routines, friends, colleges, careers, and hobbies out there just waiting for you to choose.

As you go through life, you will notice many people simply choose the spouse, college, and the career that's just good enough. But life is way too short and God's plan for your life is way too amazing for you to settle for anything that is just good enough. People and things that are excellent, awesome, and amazing are what you should be aiming for when it comes to your future.

As you journey through life, people with good intentions are going to suggest certain things, people, and jobs for you to choose. I would encourage you and challenge you – don't settle for good ideas, go after God's ideas. You do not need just any school, just any job, or just any spouse; what you need is God's best for your life. Decide you will aim high and pursue the best college, spouse, career, friends, and habits that God has specifically designed and reserved for you personally.

I assure you, the type of job and spouse you eventually choose will make all the difference in your life. If you think about it, your spouse is the only relative you have the power to choose – choose wisely. You will go to bed and wake up, raise your children, and make all of life's major decisions with him or her. You and your spouse need to be each other's best friend, biggest supporter, and closest sidekick throughout all of life's ups and downs. It is better to be single and wait for the right one than to hastily choose the wrong one and spend the rest of your life with him or her.

The choice you make when it comes to your career is also monumentally important. Although you can change your job and even your career one day, you still want to be careful regarding what you initially choose. The education and training you receive for your job will be a substantial investment of time and money and so you want to be sure the investment of time and money you make is going to pay dividends in your life someday in the future.

Seek to find a career that matches your personality, gifts, and the level of potential you believe God wants you to achieve throughout your lifetime. Yes, we have to start somewhere and there is nothing wrong with working entry level jobs when we first start out. The problem is when we become complacent and the entry level job becomes good enough even though there are unfulfilled dreams and untapped potential living inside of us.

Regarding excellent choices and aiming high, we could go on and on about friends, habits, routines, hobbies, etc. The point is, when you look at your life and the trajectory of your future, is it something God is pleased with and that you are proud of? If not, it's never too late to dream big, make room for greater things in your life, and start to move forward from where you are right now.

God wants us to live abundant, satisfying, and fulfilling lives. The only way this can be an everyday reality for us is if we are fully alive, operating on all cylinders, and being everything He has created us to be. This is why it is so critical for us to understand who we are in God, seek to know His will for our lives, and do everything we can to prepare for it and attain it.

You are God's precious child so aim high, dream big, decide you will never give up, and that you are going to do everything in your ability and power to reach your greatest potential. You are God's champion! Start believing it and living it every single day!

Day 31 Prayer of a Champion

"God, I want my life and daily routine to be pleasing to You and so please strengthen me each day to live a life of character and excellence – the life of a true champion. I pray You will cause me to dream big and aim high in every area of my life. I want to live at my very best and fulfill my destiny and so direct my steps and lead me to the amazing habits, routines, friends, colleges, careers, hobbies, and spouse you have uniquely chosen for me. Help me to not settle for just good ideas but to go after all that You are dreaming about and planning for my life. May my life and the trajectory of my future be pleasing in Your sight as well as something I am both excited about and proud of. I am Your child and I pray You will empower me to live the abundant, satisfying, and fulfilling life where I am fully alive, fulfilling my destiny, and being the champion You created me to be. Amen!"

APPENDIX

Scripture quotations marked NIV taken from HOLY BIBLE, NEW INTERNATIONAL VERSION®. Copyright © 1973, 1978, 1984 by International Bible Society. Used by permission of Zondervan Publishing House.

Scripture quotations marked NCV quoted from The Holy Bible: New Century Version®, copyright © 2005 by Thomas Nelson, Inc. Used by permission.

Scripture quotations marked GNT are from the Good News Translation in Today's English Version- Second Edition Copyright © 1992 by American Bible Society. Used by Permission.

Scripture quotations marked NLT are taken from the Holy Bible, New Living Translation, copyright © 1996, 2004, 2007 by Tyndale House Foundation. Used by permission of Tyndale House Publishers, Inc., Carol Stream, Illinois 60188. All rights reserved.

Scripture quotations marked MSG taken from THE MESSAGE. Copyright © 1993, 1994, 1995, 1996, 2000, 2001, 2002. Used by permission of NavPress Publishing Group.

Scripture quotations marked CEV are from the Contemporary English Version Copyright © 1991, 1992, 1995 by American Bible Society, Used by Permission.

Scripture quotations marked AMP taken from the Amplified® Bible, Copyright © 1954, 1958, 1962, 1964, 1965, 1987 by The Lockman Foundation. All rights reserved. Used by permission. (www.Lockman.org)

ABOUT THE AUTHOR

Active in church ministry and missions since 1998, Russ Mason is a Christian Pastor, Author, Bible Teacher, and Leadership Coach who is passionate about helping people, churches, and organizations reach their greatest potential. He and his wife Shari have been happily married since 2001 and together they have four amazing boys. Russ and Shari are the founders of The River - A Christian church, retreat, and ministry training center near Richmond, VA. Please visit russmason.org and theriverva.org for more information.

~

RUSS MASON'S OTHER BOOK TITLE

Making Disciples and Leading Small Groups

Connect with Russ Mason

Connect with Russ to receive ongoing encouragement and inspiration that will help you move forward and become everything God has created you to be!

Ministry Website
russmason.org

Ministry Facebook Page
facebook.com/russmason.org

YouTube Channel
youtube.com/user/Rmason235

LinkedIn Profile
linkedin.com/in/russ-mason-0a4b8677

The River Website
theriverva.org

River Facebook Page
facebook.com/theriverva

Email
mason235@gmail.com

Mailing Address
P.O. Box 2505 Midlothian, VA 23113

YOUR FEEDBACK IS GREATLY APPRECIATED

———————————

Thank you so much for taking time to read this book on life, excellence, and leadership. I hope it has encouraged and challenged you to be better and to reach higher!

If it has been a source of blessing and inspiration to you, I would greatly appreciate you taking a moment to leave a favorable review on the internet for others to read. Thank you for your time and I look forward to connecting with you online and maybe even meeting you one day.

Keep moving forward and may God shine brightly upon you and cause you to become everything He has created you to be!

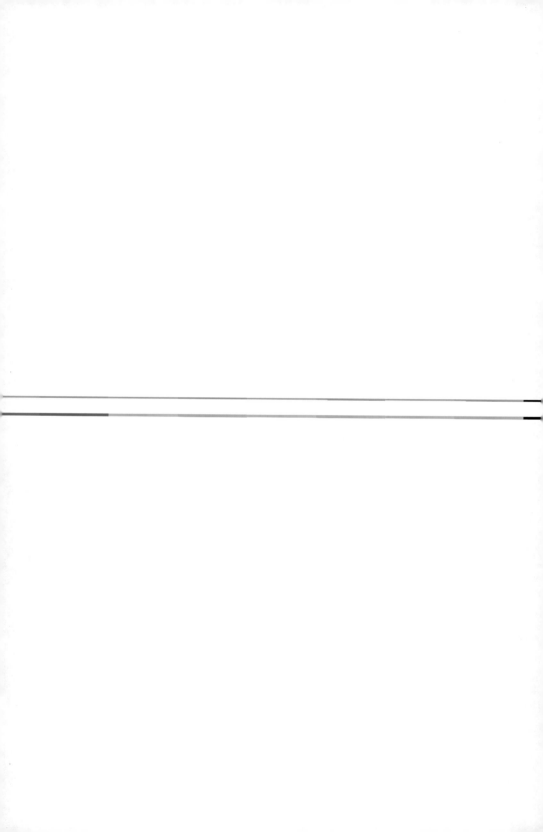